Contents

Introduction   i
The Call of the Rockies   1
Homesteading   8
A Miner at Butte   27
New Conceptions of Life   41
Years of Adventuring   50
A Crowded Pattern   64
"Colorado Snow Observer"   78
The New Inn   92
Writing and Speaking   106
Work for the Nation   124
Home Ties   141
The Last Stand   154
Appendix: Tributes   177
Comparative Obituaries   184

Daguerreotype of Enos, age 5, 1875.

Introduction

This book is just a small window into the life of Enos A. Mills. Enos did not have the expected social advantages to achieve the accomplishments that filled his life. He was successful because he did what he loved, he followed his authentic path. Enos was simply a human being, just like each one of us with human flaws and human challenges to over come. He made his choices and we now benefit from his hard work and determination to make our world a better place.

Enos' life is a basic example of what anyone may do with their life if one if one loves what they do, with those able bodied companions, honor, integrity and enthusiasm. Dear Reader, we hope you will find this book to be a catalyst for new exuberance in your own life.

Daguerreotype of Enos, age 8, 1878.

Enos A. Mills
of the Rockies

Hildegarde Hawthorne
and Esther Burnell Mills

Temporal Mechanical Press
Long's Peak, Colorado

Temporal Mechanical Press
a division of Enos Mills Cabin
6760 Highway 7
Estes Park, CO 80517-6404
www.enosmills.com

ISBN 978-1-928878-33-9

Cover photograph: Enos A. Mills on the summit of Mount of the Holy Cross.
Back cover photograph: Esther Burnell Mills, photograph by Enos A. Mills.

"During the long centuries between cave and cottage, our good ancestors traveled Nature's inspiring pictured scenes. With interest and with awe they watched the silent movements of the clouds across the sky, they listened with speechless wonder to the mysterious, unseen echo that lived and mimicked in the air, they puzzled over the strange, invisible wind that shook the excited trees and whispered in the rustling grass. They heard the echoing crash of thunder, saw lightning's golden rivers in the cloud mountains and looked with childish joy upon the silken rainbow. They marveled at the wondrous sunrise, the light of day, the fireflies in the forest, and the lonely, changing moon. The mysterious darkness was never understood, but the silent, faithful stars they named and watched with nightly wonder. By trail and campfire these thought-filled wonders took life and color, became poetic stories. Through the changing seasons and the passing years Nature built the brain and kindled the illuminating imagination—the immortal torch that guided our advancing race and which triumphantly leads us on."

Enos A. Mills.

The Pleasanton, Kansas farmhouse where Enos was born.

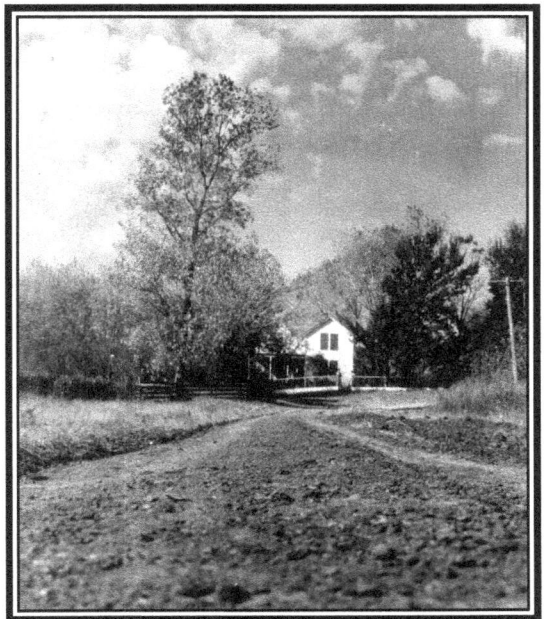

The Call of the Rockies

Work was over for the day in the white farmhouse. It had been a hot, tiring day, in the rush to finish spring planting before the rainy season descended on southeastern Kansas. As the sun dipped below the horizon, a breeze sprang up, rustling the leaves of the dusty old cottonwood with a refreshing sound. The small boy seated on the top step of the porch sighed with content. He found a peculiar, deep satisfaction in being alone and out-of-doors.

The still early twilight revealed the child's face and figure. The thick, close-cropped hair was reddish and showed a tendency to curl over the finely shaped head with its broad, high forehead. It was an intelligent, sensitive face, with a suggestion of suffering, of ill health that had sculptured the cheeks to hollowness, and accentuated the modeling of the firm mouth and chin. The peace of the evening stole into his being and his features relaxed into an expression of boyish happiness.

The clatter of voices and dishes from the kitchen reminded him that the family were still at supper. He had little appetite for the slice of bread and butter with which he must begin each meal at his father's insistence. This was before the day of dietetics, and his dislike of what the rest of the family ate with relish was attributed to a streak of stubbornness rather than to its true cause—a weak digestion. He had tried to choke down the food put before him, but without success, and, at a nod from his mother, had slipped away unnoticed.

The boy was Enos Mills and the year was 1884. As he sat alone in the oncoming darkness he was dreaming of faraway Colorado—that land of promise for the prospector, the trapper, the hunter, and mountain explorer. For which occupation, he wondered, would he be fitted? Of pioneer parents, who had tracked from South Bend, Indiana, to Iowa with an ox-team in the '50s, then shortly moved on to Kansas, he had been brought up to the rigors of hardship and toil. For farming, he realized, he was scarcely suited, that a life in the open where he could be on his own—

His dreaming was interrupted by a voice in the doorway:

"You there, Tom?"

"Yes, Ma." He answered to the nickname which was used by the family to distinguish him from his father, whose name had been given him at his birth, April 22, 1870.

Mrs. Mills slipped noiselessly into a low rocker and began to hum softly to herself. The boy came and leaned against her knee, for this was the one hour of the day they could talk together, while his sisters cleared away the suppers things and his father was busy with the papers brought once a week from Fort Scott, 20 miles away.

"Ma, tell me about Colorado," implored the boy, unwilling to waste a minute of the precious time.

"Now, Tom, what makes you keep thinking about the Rockies; ain't it nice enough right here in the cool of the evening? How those crickets are chirping! Well, let's see, what do you want I should tell you?"

"About that time you and Pa went up the gulch prospecting and you met a big grizzly coming down."

"How you do remember, child! I guess you could almost tell it yourself," his mother chuckled softly, enjoying the enthusiasm of the boy resting against her.

"There were tall pine trees swaying in the breeze and you were watching the big white clouds moving across the bright blue sky," Enos continued, to recall her memory.

"Yes, and your pa used to say I never would find gold if I didn't stop picking wild flowers. But each one was more beautiful than the last: blue, gold, red, purple flowers growing wild all over those mountains—how I loved them! We had planned to pitch camp beside a beautiful mountain stream, but thought we would look around a bit. I wish you could just taste that wonderful pure mountain water; it makes me right thirsty just to think of it. And how the stars shown at night, after we rolled up in our blankets!" Her thoughts wandered off to twenty-five years before, when as a girl in her early twenties she had followed her husband in the gold rush of '59 to the mountains of Colorado.

"Breckenridge, wasn't it, Ma? Are they still prospecting there, do you think? Is there any work a boy my age could do?"

"It's no work for a boy, Tom, prospecting ain't. Even your father gave it up after a few months. With all that digging, he

At Left:
Enos Mills Sr. and
Ann Lamb Mills.

Mills Family portrait. Top row from left: Enos Abijah,
Sarah, Belle and Ella. Bottom row: Enoch (Joe),
Naomi, Ann Lamb Mills, Enos Mills Sr. and Horace.

said, a body might as well be plowing Kansas prairies. Crops were surer than outcrops to his way of thinking. But that mountain air sure is fine, and such appetites as we had! I believe even you would be able to eat out there. Seems to me you're getting thinner and thinner the way you pick at your victuals."

"I ain't hungry, Ma; seems like something tells me not to eat when I don't want to."

"I know, but you won't grow if you don't eat. And your father expects you to do a man's work, though you ain't as big even as a twelve-year-old boy. Maybe it would be better for you to go to Colorado. There's lots doing out there now according to all accounts, folks going out for the scenery and hunting. There ought to be work of some kind. And you'd like it fine, those high peaks piled with snow, glowing like rubies when the sun first strikes them."

He stood straight, his hands clenched in a sudden determination. "That's what I think, too. And I'm going, going tomorrow!"

The conversation was interrupted by his sisters joining them.

"What's Horace doing, Bell?" asked Mrs. Mills.

"El's helping him with his arithmetic."

Mrs. Mills rose, giving Enos a pat on the arm. She was a frail-looking woman, small of stature, weighing less than a hundred pounds, but wiry and active and of unbounded endurance.

"You girls rest a spell. I'll go put little Joe to bed, if he ain't already asleep by now. Beats all how the time goes." She went into the house singing softly to herself, as she thought of her big family, four girls and three boys. The youngest, Enoch Joe, now nearly five, was later to follow his brother to Colorado. Of a happy disposition, Mrs. Mills did not worry overmuch about young Enos, knowing instinctively that his destiny was beyond her controlling. Hers was not a nature to hold her children too closely to her, once their longing reached beyond the home nest, and Enos especially had ever been restless among this brood of noisy, chattering children, seeking solitude in the quiet of the prairie reaches whenever he could steal the time away from farm duties.

Sarah and Bell soon tired of the darkened landscape and, the meager news of the day exhausted, followed their mother into the house and joined the family circle under the hanging kerosene lamp. There was always sewing to be done in this big family and the evenings were profitably employed.

Naomi lingered on the porch with Enos.

"Were you and Ma talking about Colorado?" she presently asked.

"Say, Sis, do you think a boy my age could get work out there?" he questioned eagerly.

"That's just what I wanted to tell you. I have the address of a summer place where people go to hunt and fish and enjoy the mountains. Here it is; 'Estes Park' is the name of it," handing him a slip of paper. "Keep that and, when you get a chance to go, maybe it will be worth knowing."

"Thanks, Sis. I'll ask when I get to Denver City how to go there. I'm sure I'll be better in Colorado than here. And I'm not much help, anyway, except with horses. Pa says I do have a real knack with them. If I didn't have to miss so much school I wouldn't mind the work. Can I take some of those school-books of yours, so I can study when I get to feeling better? A boy has to have an education if he gets ahead in the world."

"Shucks, child, you don't need to worry. 'Where there's a will, there's a way,' you know. I believe you'll make your way all right. When do you think you will go?"

"Tomorrow, perhaps."

"Tomorrow," echoed his mother from the doorway.

The boy turned and their eyes met in a long look, bright with the glitter of tears. But a smile was on the woman's lips as she turned back into the house. Deep within her she was content.

When next day the sun rose, sending long shadows over the still sleeping land, it shone on a small figure plodding northward, a bundle on his back that held all his possessions, a few articles of clothing, the cherished books, and a lunch of fried chicken and dried fruit which his mother knew he liked. It was some ninety miles to Kansas city, toward which the boy had set his face, in the hope of finding work until he could save enough to buy a ticket to Denver City. He was going to the Rockies and the idea carried him on. His was the indomitable spirit of pioneer Kansas.

As early as the beginning years of the fifties, the early influx of settlers into the State consisted to a large degree of people possessed by an idea, the idea of human freedom; they wanted no slaves on Kansas soil. They fought for that principle as wholeheartedly, as fiercely, as they fought the climate when it turned against them, as it often did, bringing a year or years of drought after seasons of rain and fruitfulness. Terrific winters came after burning summers, but the stout-hearted endured, conquering even the elements, turning the prairie into wheat and cornfields, raising horses and cattle, building substantial homes, planting trees on those treeless plains, digging wells so deep no drought could exhaust them. The farms reached back to villages; these grew to towns; schools were established for the growing children that they might be better educated than the hard-pressed elders had been; meeting houses gathered the Godfearing to hear the Word. A fanatical people, possibly, but willing to suffer and to work for their ideas and their ideals; proud of the land to which they had come, learning to love it for the very difficulties with which it opposed them.

Enos was setting his short stride against Fate. He was taking the first steps on the long trail that was to lead him, not only to the summit of the highest peaks in his country, but to heights of achievement and renown that would have appeared, from that farm and springtime of 1884, far more inaccessible.

The days passed, not unpleasantly for Enos. It was great to be in the open alone, and where there was no hurry and no need to eat if he wasn't hungry. Sometimes he had a supper and bed in a farmhouse, helping with the chores so numerous around evening, and which he knew so well. Sometimes he had a lift of a few miles in a farm wagon, and good advice in the bargain.

"So you're trampin' to Denver City? Better take a shotgun to keep off the Injins!"

"Oh, I 'spect I could scare 'em without that," Enos would answer.

For two days he took shelter out of pouring rain in a friendly farmhouse, where he was pressed to stay longer if he wished. He was handy around the house, inside as well as out, and willing beyond reason. He had no hard-luck story to tell; rather he spoke of amusing or interesting happenings along the way, his impressions of the changing scenery and the flowers and birds that never escaped him. When he declared his destination as Colorado, the elderly couple were especially interested. Their son had gone to the Rockies, and they hoped sometime to join him. In parting they gave Enos the address of friends in Kansas City who might help him find work.

And so it proved. Although it was several days before he was able to located a job as a baker's errand boy, they helped him find his way around the city, which was a bit terrifying to a country lad, unfamiliar with the hustle and bustle of the streets. He found the baker exceedingly strict and particular, and he was called down pretty sharply for the slightest mistake. But it was all good training, and he never made the same mistake twice.

Eventually, he walked proudly out of the railroad station with a ticked to Denver City in his pocket. The realization that he was actually to ride on the train was almost more than he could believe. He walked block after block in his excitement, then fearing lest he would miss the train started to run back to the station. He still had an hour to wait, and with nothing else to occupy his time, took out his copy of the "Manual of the Constitution of the United States," by Israel Ward Andrews, "Designed for the Instruction of American Youth in the Duties, Obligations, and Rights of Citizenship."

"All aboard!" brought him quickly to his feet. And in the next moment, it seemed, the train whistled, jerked, started. He drew a long breath, pulled his head inside the window, and settled in his seat. He was on his way to the Rockies!

Homesteading

"Go where you will into the Rocky Mountains and the birds will greet and cheer you. They will make you feel the spell of living. Peaks, plateaus, snowfields, forests, canyons, meadows, lakes, and streams—each has its busy, happy bird people. A number are mountain residents, others are trailers of the Sun. Grace, beauty, and song place them in the world of art; bird songs are a part of the music of existence."

Enos A. Mills

"Is there any land around here not took up yet?" Enos asked. It was June, 1885.

"Well, I reckon there's land enough for a boy your size. Figuring on doing a little prospecting, be ye?" asked the Reverend Elkanah Lamb, shifting his corncob pipe as he eyed the small boy quizzically.

"I don't know as I'd prospect, exactly. Just want to have a cabin of my own here in the mountains. Want to be where I can see Long's Peak every day, and climb it too. When I'm old enough, I'll file a claim, have a homestead. I don't know of any place I'd rather live than right here, in this valley."

"Sure, that's what everyone thinks the first time they come here. I'll never forget my first impression of Long's Peak. It was a sight sublime to the eye and almost solemn to contemplate, as an example of God's handiwork. It ain't so easy to climb, though, as you'd think. You'd never guess it's over fourteen thousand feet high; just how high nobody knows exactly, but more than a mile higher than this valley. And it's a rough climb, too, over rocks and boulders, after you get above that green stretch of timber. And that east precipice! It gives me nightmares every time I think of the time in 1871 when I descended it!"

"Were you alone?" asked Enos.

"Yes, I left the rest of the party on top, saying I'd just make a try at it, anyway. But after I got down a way I couldn't go back, so nothing for it but to keep on going down. It's a wonder I ever came out alive. Just the grace of God spared me, I reckon."

Enos with the housekeeping staff at Elkhorn Lodge.
The women are unidentified.

Enos with women at Elkhorn Lodge.

"But you liked the country?" Enos questioned.

"Sure, the memory of those forests and flowers stayed with me. Never was satisfied until I put the family in a wagon and came back four years later. But it took us two weeks to chop a wagon road in. That was pioneering with a vengeance. The Fergusons came in the same year, but they never got farther than Mary's Lake. That satisfied them, maybe. But not me. I like scenery, plenty of it, and this Long's Peak Valley sure has the best. But homesteading, now, for a boy your size, I ain't so sure it's practical. How old are you?"

"Fifteen," Enos answered. "But I've been in Colorado a year now and like it fine. Worked at Elkhorn Lodge last summer. But this suits me better than Estes Park; it's closer to Long's Peak."

"So you've been down at Elkhorn, have you? That's some hotel; attracts a lot of tourists. Them Jameses are sure some hunters. What'd you do, help stack those elkhorns? I hear that's their real showpiece."

"I didn't have much time for that. I kept busy with dish-washing and wood chopping, carrying the mail, helping out in the commissary, and even serving the ladies afternoon tea!"

"Mighty interesting, I expect, but that don't make no mountaineer of you. Some job tackling these hills, winter and summer, as my son Carlyle can tell you. He's running the ranch here, and a mighty big job it is, too, rounding up cattle, guiding parties up Long's Peak, hauling supplies eight miles by team, clearing the timber, and trying to hustle a living. My place is a mile north, 'Mountain Home' we call it. I come down to help Carlyle out a bit now and then."

"But I know ranch work, too," Enos hastened to explain. "I spent last winter out in eastern Colorado, where the winter's worse than it is here, they tell me. There wasn't much I didn't try my hand at, from logging to tending the baby Sunday evenings when the Smiths went to church. I can go back again next winter, if I want, but I figure on staying here in the mountains. Just seeing Long's from the plains ain't enough for me."

"So you've handled logs, have you? Well, that's some tough job. Say, Carlyle," calling through the doorway of the kitchen, "here's just the person you've been waiting for, to help clear out this stand of timber you've been wanting for some more pasture."

A man of about twenty-five came to the door, sparse of frame but not so tall as his more than six-foot father. Introductions over, in the deliberate mountain manner Enos stated his purpose again.

"I'm looking for a cabin site. I like that spot over yonder," pointing to a stretch of half-open slope across the brook from the Lamb's ranch, "where I'd have the mountain back of me and Long's Peak always before me. Logs of Douglas Spruce over there, too, just right for building logs. And there's a spring close by."

"Well, I reckon there ain't nothing to hinder," Carlyle answered. "It ain't been claimed yet. That hundred and sixty lies next to my place here and on south across Kit Carson Brook. Nothing on it but beaver that I know of. But building a cabin, I'll tell you, ain't so easy. And what'd you do with it? Can't live alone, can you?"

"One ain't never alone in the mountains. They're always friendly some way, and they understand you, too, seem to welcome you, I think." Enos gazed longingly up at Long's Peak as he spoke, wishing he had the strength to make the steep, difficult ascent. Then, turning toward Twin Sisters Peaks with the green-clad slopes reaching up gently to a broken, rocky skyline, his gaze encompassed that splendid sweep of valley that had taken such a hold on his imagination and his plans for the future.

"Beats all how the mountains do get hold of one," Lamb agreed, "though I can't say they're very profitable. Season's too short for tourists or cultivating, either one. Scenery sure don't grow victuals."

"Seems to me I could live on air and scenery," Enos said. "I mean to climb Long's Peak some day, and all the rest of these peaks."

"Well, you take a hand around and maybe Carlyle can give you a lift with the log cutting by and by. One man can't do it alone, let alone a mere boy. If you can handle horses, you might go out and harness up the team. I've got to go to the village for supplies."

Enos went to the barn where he harnessed up the team in

short order, and had it ready and waiting for Mr. Lamb. He had a way with animals that always won them, and he especially liked horses.

Lamb's Ranch was a substantial log building, standing about in the center of the valley, beside a small mountain stream. The valley was well watered from the surrounding slopes, and the thick meadow grass had been cleared for a garden patch within an enclosure fenced with poles. As in all new settlements trees were rapidly cleared to make room for pasture, and stock roamed at large over the surrounding country.

The western side of the valley sloped up in gradual ascents to the summit of Long's Peak that lifted its split crest against the sky, a bare and rocky giant. The encircling mountains drained southward to the St. Vrain River, while Estes Park lay northward eight miles, and fifteen hundred feet lower.

Few tourists came into the valley as yet, as it was considered too remote and inaccessible. But the Lambs were hospitable and welcomed those who came up from Estes Park to spend a night and have the Reverend Elkanah Lamb or Carlyle guide them up the Peak. Occasional parties came in from Denver, Boulder, Longmont, Loveland, or Greeley, with a team and provisions, and "tented" along the streams or at timberline, two thousand feet higher. They saw the country at its best, and though the traveling was slow and sometimes difficult, vacations were enjoyed with more regard for leisure and less for speed than is true today.

The earliest tourists 1867-77, among them Professor F. V. Hayden, Anna E. Dickinson—the first woman to ascend Long's Peak—Isabella Bird, Albert Bierstadt, the artist, and Lord Dunraven with his English friends had been accommodated at Evan's Ranch—the old Joel Estes claim, on Fish Creek, at the eastern entrance to the Estes Park Valley.

At Lamb's Ranch, Enos found the usual duties to keep a boy busy. Always there was wood to provide for the big fireplace; horses, cows, chickens, and pigs to be fed and cared for; water to be brought from the spring; churning, dish-washing, and errands all over the place. As tourists came and went, Enos thrilled with their accounts of climbing Long's Peak, forming, however, his own conception of what it would mean to see the world from the top. Finally the opportunity came for him to accompany Carlyle, and help with the heavy cameras the party were taking along.

Breakfast was served at four o'clock: ham and eggs, coffee and gems. At five o'clock the party was under way. It was a day of excitement to the boy of fifteen, who had so long dreamed of this great adventure. The description which follows is taken from his "Story of Estes Park and a Guide Book," published twenty years later.

"The trail winds away up the mountainside, alongside a bustling stream, through a forest green and grand. The stream has all the characteristics of Southey's 'Cataract of Lodore.' Here it leaps over rocks, there it lingers in quiet pools, lined with shining sand and fringed with ferns; then rushes impetuously down a cascade and hurries away through flowery dells, beneath the forest's shade.

"The trail next crosses a mineral outcrop, where miners 'in days of old' have delved for gold and glory.

"At an altitude of 11,000 feet, timberline is reached. What a weird scene! Here for ages has been the line of battle between the woods and weather. Many of the trees are destitute of both bark and limbs on the western side, the direction of the storms. All the trees are broken, twisted, and dwarfed; some of them are several inches in diameter and only a few inches in height; others grow along the ground, forming hideous looking vines, creeping away from the direction of the storms, retreating from life's awful battle.

"Just above timberline are snowfields, embroidered with flowers, where works the busy bee and where the butterfly spreads its painted sails above the petals. Higher up are grassy slopes and rocky ridges, the home of the mountain sheep.

"On Boulderfield, at an altitude of 12,500 feet, the horses are left behind. Boulderfield is a field of about one thousand acres, covered with slabs of granite and boulders of gneiss. Some of the rocks are forty feet in length, and all, both great and small, are thrown together in utmost confusion. It is the source of many brooks and the home of ptarmigan. Here also grow columbines, gentians, paintbrushes, and many other flowers.

"One mile from the summit is 'Keyhole,' a ragged break

through the partition of granite that divides Boulderfield from Glacier Gorge. A peep through Keyhole reveals a scene at once awful and magnificent. It is the end of Glacier Gorge expanded into a gigantic amphitheater and is filled with lakes, cliffs, spires, and winter's drifted snow. Some of the lakes are frozen, some of them reflect the snow cornices of the over-hanging cliffs. The sides of the canyon seem a network of silvery streams, where 'the wild cataracts leaps in glory.' Lower down in the canyon are many dark lakes nestling in the forest green. The prospect from here fills one with the those intense feelings that go with views from Artists' Point, Point Lookout, or the Canyon of the Colorado.

"Beyond the 'Keyhole' the trail winds away along a narrow ledge fringed with Greek valerian that lure their color from the sky. About one thousand feet from the summit the trail toils up the 'trough,' a gully in granite, about twelve hundred feet in length, and inclined at an angle of about thirty-five degrees. The 'Trough' is connected by the 'Narrows' to the 'Home-stretch.' Here grows the alpine primrose, with its petals of fire. The 'Homestretch' is a granite slope, as steep as a house roof. In doing this the climber finds the balance of breath decidedly against him. The 'Homestretch' ends at the 'Summit'.

"The top is an almost level surface of granite slabs and about three hundred by six hundred feet, and is inaccessible from two sides. On the east is a precipice of 2500 feet, almost perpendicular for 1200 feet. At the bottom of the wall, about 3000 feet from the top, lies Chasm Lake, surrounded on three sides by high walls, with an outlet through a deep canyon that plainly shows the polish and scars of glacier erosion. This canyon is an excellent place to study fracture and flexure. On the banks are enormous lateral moraines that wind away until lost in the woods.

"To the north, Estes Park unfolds its beauty, with trees sprinkled here and there and many a winding stream. To the west and south great numbers of lakes huddle near the Peak, and there are numerous canyons inlaid with ice, with their sides gnawed into fantastic shapes by wind and water. To the east, just beyond the foothills, the plains are checkered with fields of green and gold, and far out is the Platte River, loitering here and there in groves of green, then plowing its way across the plains. To the southeast stands Denver. One hundred miles away to the southeast stands Pike's Peak, like a sky-touching pyramid. Northwest in Wyoming, Laramie Peak mingles its dim, silvery summit with the clouds. Southwest, Mount Holy Cross goes up into the sky.

"To the west is Middle Park, through which the Grand (Colorado) River hurried on its course to the sea. On the north, timbered mountains stretch away until they meet the bending blue. On the southwest, range after range of snow-capped peaks roll and toss away like foam-crowned billows of the deep, while on every side streams rise and ribbon themselves seaward. What a roof garden is the pile of rusty rocks! What sun-tipped peaks and gloomy canyons, flowery fields and wooded wilds advance upon the scene!"

There were nights when the ranch house was overflowing with guests, and on such occasions Enos gave up his bed and spread his blankets in the hayloft. It occurred to him that if he had even the beginning to his cabin, it would often serve to good purpose.

But Carlyle, who had promised to assist him, was busy in a hundred ways throughout August and Enos finally went to work alone with his axe. He had selected the trees carefully, one here and there among the denser growths, where they would not be missed, mature Douglas spruce that were sound and tough. That the little cabin still stands today, over one hundred years later, is proof of his wise selection.

"You'll find it tough work," Lamb remarked one day when he came upon Enos in the woods; "felling trees ain't so easy as you think."

Enos nodded. He hadn't imagined it would be easy. If it were possible, that would be as much as he expected.

The tough spruce resisted the axe obstinately. This was arduous labor for a man; for an undersized and not too robust boy, accomplished only with severest difficulty. But tree by tree Enos won.

It took a great many logs to build even a small cabin. He had marked out the inside dimensions at twelve by fourteen feet, and decided the walls should be about eight feet high. That required nine logs each, for all four sides. All these logs must be cut the right length, then deeply notched at both ends and both sides to fit firmly into each other.

Autumn came early with an unusual snowstorm and the Lambs began preparations to move their stock out for the winter. They thought Enos would abandon his plans. Instead, he borrowed a horse and dragged the felled trees down to the spot selected for his cabin. With the second snowfall of the season, the Lambs packed up and left for their winter home at Fort Collins.

"We'll leave you some grub so you won't starve for a while," Mr. Lamb said in parting, "and perhaps next summer we can pay you wages. Mountains ain't so profitable for a living, boy, but I see the beaver doing some cutting downstream; maybe you can get a few skins to help out for the winter."

The weather turned mild and with ordinary luck Enos would have made considerable progress. One of his attacks of indigestion occurred and he was too weak to lift the heavy logs into place. Stones had been laid for the corners and the ground leveled up in readiness for the building. But it would have to wait.

He had built a lean-to of boughs and sod to answer his temporary requirements. One night as he lay rolled up in his blankets beside a little campfire, a peculiar sound reached his ears.

"Chip, chip, chip."

It sounded as though someone were cutting his trees.

Rising on an elbow, he listened again. The aspen grove stood out distinctly in the bright moonlight, but no one was to be seen. Presently one of the taller trees caught his attention. It swayed as though being gently shaken. It was all very mysterious. Then a small, dark figure at the ground moved around the tree and stood up against the tree trunk. A beaver!

Wide, wide awake now, and all alert, Enos lay still and watched to see how long it would take the beaver to finish the cutting. The tree was swaying more and more. Two nips, it seemed, the beaver took on the far side of the tree and over it went with a thud. The next move of the beaver was to cut off the smaller branches. It moved silently and deliberately, taking its time. An owl hooted nearby, but the beaver gave no sign that it heard. When the tree was neatly trimmed, it set to work cutting the trunk into sections. Occasionally it took a bite of bark and chewed it. Stopping for lunch, Enos thought to himself.

Enos watched without a move, while the beaver continued his cutting until a two-foot section of the aspen trunk lay on the ground. Apparently the beaver had plans for it. Rolling it away from the fallen tree, he dug his teeth into it and dragged it slowly, noiselessly, down the slope to the water's edge. There was hardly a ripple as the beaver and the log slid into the water. Far off a coyote called, then another and another.

Tense with the excitement of the show he had been watching, the weird note of the coyote made Enos shiver. Not that he was afraid; he had seen and heard coyotes often enough. But would it be safe for the beaver to come back to his tree cutting? At any rate, the beaver did not come back, for when daylight came the cutting had not been finished.

It was a long time before the boy could go to sleep. He was thinking of his little cabin, wishing he could work out some scheme to get the task further along. He thought of the beaver and the "job" he had just completed.

"I know," he said, half aloud; "he works slowly, easily, as though he did not have to hurry. Perhaps I am in too big a rush and go at it too hard." It was a happy thought, which soon put him to sleep, to dream of a beaver cutting the notches in his logs and dragging them into place.

The boy approached his work the next day with new courage. He viewed his pile of logs with admiration; they were his logs and they were going into his cabin. Picking up the axe, he swung it a few times in the air to limber up his arms. Then he tried it on a block of wood to get a sure drive. Turning to the logs, he rolled one into place, smoothed it down slightly with his axe to give a level surface. Next it was notched at the corner where the cross-log would fit upon it. He was sure at this point the beaver would stop and rest, and, feeling elated over his work, he walked off upstream to view the beaver work. Their house of mud and willow branches was already completed. A few floating green aspen—their winter food supply—were accumulating. Though he sometimes saw the animals in the daytime, working on the house or dam, the tree cutting seemed all to be done at night.

The days went swiftly for Enos; the laying and fitting of his logs was absorbing and he was delighted to find that he was able to put in a few hours of work each day without becoming exhausted. The rest of the time he put in at the beaver pond, watching their food gathering progress night by night. Sometimes he would see the beaver lazily swimming about in the pond, or leisurely eating on the side of the house. They did not appear to be worrying about the weather or the food supply.

Waking one morning in mid-October, Enos found the ground already white and the snow falling heavily. He knew it was time to leave his work and go to other scenes for the winter. But next year, with good luck, he would have his cabin finished to live in. He lugged his tools and few personal possessions over to the Lambs' barn and stowed them carefully away.

His immediate concern was now finding work for the winter. He knew of a cattle ranch in eastern Colorado where he might be taken on. Gathering together his few possessions, including his precious arithmetic, he started out for new scenes and experiences. The work would be hard, the foreman had warned him, but would give him an opportunity to live the life of the cowboy.

Enos was a curious mixture of the wanderer and the home lover. From the moment when he chose the site of Homestead Cabin until his death, it was home to him, the dearest spot on earth. It gave him the opportunity to live in the mountains, to rove over the country, to observe without hurry the nature that he loved. For this freedom he was willing to pay in months of labor, and the payment was genuine, full measure, pressed down and running over.

Mills liked the cowboys, and they liked him. Being the youngest of the crew, he was often the target for their jokes and pranks. But if his inexperience got him into trying situations, his sense of humor and good common sense came to his rescue.

March saw him back at his cabin and at work. His most serious problem was to work out some scheme whereby he could hoist the higher logs into place. As he worked on the building log by log, he was studying over the situation before he actually came to it. He was still alone up there in the Long's Peak Valley, hoping to get his cabin finished in order to live in it that summer.

He often paused in his work to stroll down the beaver stream, where all was quiet. The ponds were full and overflowing with the rush of water from melting snow banks higher up on the mountains. But the dams held intact, marvelous examples of permanent construction. Enos was impressed with the incidental purpose which these several dams served, in breaking the force of the swift mountain streams and preventing rapid erosion of the channel. Some of the old, abandoned beaver ponds gave evidence of rich soil that had been deposited to become meadow again. There was much time to reflect on his daily observations, and much material close at hand to arouse his curiosity and interest.

As the cabin rose higher and higher, log by log, Enos solved the problem of how to contrive a block and tackle. Several experiments were tried before he was successful. Days were spent in work which two men would have accomplished in a few hours. He was never discouraged; he was determined to master the obstacles.

Often he stopped to rest and watch the arrival of new birds on the scene. The red-winged blackbirds were the first to come, and merrily their "o-ka-lee" rang out across the marsh land. Then a pair of bluebirds appeared and lingered around the cabin. His deliberate movements seemed not to disturb them; in fact, they seemed interested in the building of the cabin.

For the structure began to take on the semblance of a cabin. An opening had been left in the west side for a window, facing the Peak. The doorway looked south into a grove of aspen with big yellow pine scattered through it. The ridge pole was finally put in place after days of effort, and after that it was a simple manner to lay poles from the walls to the ridge log to be covered with boughs and sod until better roofing could be acquired. The north gable end was closed in upright logs, and only the front of the cabin remained to be finished. To be sure, there was no floor as yet, but this might have to wait until another season. Soon he would be living in his cabin.

He left his work one day to follow a pair of goldfinches, the first he had ever seen. Their happy notes and merry chatter as they flitted about delighted him and led him on and on. When he returned to his cabin, he found the bluebirds had taken possession. After due consideration they had apparently decided that the ridge log was the safest place they could find for their nest. Mrs. Bluebird was doing most of the work, weaving dried grass into the structure with the deftness of an artist.

Enos stood and watched her in delight. Occasionally Mr. Bluebird brought material which she accepted, but sometimes he, too, only watched. In the weeks that the bluebirds had been about, Enos had already come to love them; they had become friends and companions in the wilds, and now they had come to live with him! He had no thought of disturbing the nest building, not even if the front of the cabin would have to go unfinished for a time. He gave himself up completely now to watching bluebird ways, their daily life became his. Although Mrs. Bluebird would defiantly hurl herself at any other intruder that came on the premises, Enos was allowed to go in and out of the cabin without notice. Such confidence was appealing, and he respected it to the utmost. The nest was finally completed, and five light blue eggs were laid.

※※※

Enos started out one early June day to walk to timberline on Long's Peak. With raisins and chocolate in his pocket, he was as happy as a boy off to a circus. The trail was wilder then; one might meet any of the numerous wild animals inhabiting the mountains, and he did not intend to miss anything. He went slowly, stopping to watch a new bird, enjoy a squirrel's chattering, or examine fresh deer tracks. Long he sat by the cascades, listening to the water ouzel's rich melody, seeing the bird skim under the dashing spray, but failing to discover the nest. At timberline he studied the dwarfed trees that had been twisted into strange forms in their battle for life. He saw for the first time the myriad early summer alpine flowers that covered the rocky uplands. Globe flowers and marsh marigolds crowded the snowdrifts, and tiny pink moss campion and purple phlox were massed in such profusion that he could scarcely step without treading upon them. He lay down and looked into their tiny faces, wondering how anything so small could be so perfect. The fragrant rock jasmine clustered beside glorious alpine sunflowers; alpine avens and dainty heather vied with one another for his attention. He did not know their names then, but each left an indelible impression, and filled his thoughts with a newly awakened interest.

The long shadows of the peaks were casting darkness into the valley below when Enos realized that if he was to reach home before dark he would have to start at once. But the rich glow of the sunset on elevated ridges, filling the sky with glory, held him enchanted. Suddenly the marvelous song of the solitaire broke the silence. He did not know what manner of bird it was, and it was long before he learned. Never to be forgotten was that rich melody as matchless as the setting was wild and beautiful. Long it lingered in his consciousness, clear and wild, a song full of inspiration, hope, and happiness that echoed a deep response in his own soul.

The scenes around him became friendly, the gnarled and battered timberline trees stood out like sentinels against the approach of night, the soft hush of twilight beckoned him to linger. It would be a new experience, at any rate, sleeping out under the stars up closer to the sky than he had ever slept before, Long's Peak calmly watching over the scene, so close it seemed as though he could reach out his hand and touch it.

A shelter was found in the lee of a group of dwarfed, matted spruce, that crouched against a huge boulder. His fire was quickly burning, sending forth bits of brightness into the night. It was only the first of many a campfire to be made at the end of a day in the open, wherever the night found him. But no place did he love so much, or return to so frequently, as that timberline realm of the heights, where the trees make their last stand against the elements and alpine flowers possess the rocky meadows.

Waking before dawn he watched the first light come slowly, saw the first crimson flush touch the Peak, the drop downward gradually, until all the mountain was bathed in light. Again the song of the solitaire broke the stillness and he was enraptured anew. How friendly was the scene, the strange timberline trees like old acquaintances, the flowers that greeted him, the wind that whispered in the pines far down the slope. He was no longer alone.

Breakfast was never much of a ceremony with Enos, and this morning it was less of one than usual; a few raisins and the last of his chocolate. But he was happy, doing what he wanted to do, free to linger and enjoy the magic of that June day in his own way. At length he started homeward, down through the forest aisles of fir, spruce, and pine, where the brook sparkled and tumbled and flowers filled every open sunny glade. Here the hermit thrush sang, and the gray jay came close to the trail, a startled deer sprang gracefully into the forest depths.

It was good to have the bluebirds greet him when he arrived at his cabin, and it was fine to be home! His one room, with its homemade bench and table, its shelves with his few books and belongings, the bluebird nest over the ridge log, the smell of the pines through the window, and Long's Peak watching over all, gave him a deep sense of content; it was not so much a feeling that it all belonged to him, as that he belonged to it.

There was not much that he could do on his cabin while the bluebirds were nesting, but he chinked the logs inside and out, and made the frames for the door and window. He helped out at times at the Lambs' and worked with Carlyle on the trail, making it easier for horses. And with watching the bluebirds, making friends with the squirrels and chipmunks around the cabin, and exploring up and down the beaver stream, his summer was more than full.

The bluebirds raised two broods that summer and Enos became well acquainted with their family life, the feeding and training of bluebird babies, and the devotion of their parents. He also saw much of the life of other birds that came to that mountain region to nest and raise their young, and he was impressed with the varied characteristics of the different species. The quiet bluebird ever remained to him the symbol of loving trust and devotion.

For the most part he enjoyed the freedom of more leisure than he had had since coming to the mountains. He put in hours at his arithmetic, his grammar and history, mastering the rudiments of an education. His health was still far from good, but he conserved his energies, learning gradually how to climb, taking his time, resting when he felt like it, lingering long over any unusual interest. He explored the slope above his cabin, knew all the trees, their characteristics, if not their names. He was advancing in knowledge of natural history much faster than he realized.

The Lambs went out of the valley in early September, as usual, but Enos decided to stay on indefinitely. He had added a stove to his meager furnishings, and a canvas over the doorway and window space would give ample protection against storms. He wanted to give closer attention to the beaver this fall, study their tree cutting and other activities. If necessary when winter came he would find work of some kind; he was not given to worrying much about the future. It was enough just to be living in those glorious September days, with his cabin almost completed as a friendly shelter between him and the world. A trip to Estes Park occasionally gave him some contact with the other settlers and their solicitous questions.

"You ain't aimin' to stay up there all alone all winter?" John Cleave would ask, as Enos made his purchases of provisions. "You'll get snowed in or starve up there. Better stay in the village."

Enos was interested in seeing more of the mountains in winter. It was then that the deer and elk and mountain sheep came lower, feeling secure in their complete possession of the valleys. He was not going about his study systematically as yet, but reveling in the sheer adventure of covering new territory and gaining increasing confidence in his ability to meet untried conditions.

Late in the season Enos returned to the ranch on the plains for a few months, to get funds ahead for summer. As spring came on, with its wealth of flower and bird life, he went off for a camping trip, with an amateur's elaborate equipment. He visited prairie dogs that yapped at him excitedly as he stopped to view their thickly populated towns. Antelopes showed themselves occasionally, coyotes ran off on the trail of jack-rabbits, and all was life, movement and excitement for a boy. He tells the story in "Waiting in the Wilderness" in the chapter "Camping on the Plains." He learned much of value, especially about the art of camping.

From the plains the distant Continental Divide was ever a sign and a wonder. Sometimes it was cloud covered and illusive; on clear days, its sharp-cut horizon drew like a magnet. By early summer Enos was back at his cabin, and before many days had climbed Long's Peak, alone. Again he thrilled to the feeling of adventure, exulted in the view from the top, finding all the wonders of his first climb and much more. He saw the Peak now in the light of what it would mean to others; he must bring people to it. It would be worth while being a guide on this majestic peak. From that moment he determined to give the Peak his devoted study; he would learn every inch of the trail, know it at night and in fog, discover the best time one should make in climbing it, and all the points where ice or loose rocks sometimes made it necessary for careless people to be told to watch their step.

There was much more, to this boy of seventeen, in gaining the height than the mere conquering of a difficult ascent. He remained for hours in an exaltation of the spirit that matched the lofty isolation in which he stood. About him the world dropped away in beauty, a silence more thrilling than any music, hushed space and time. To the mountain lover had come the mountain's greatest gift, bringing ecstasy and awe, the sublime revelation of the heights, where man may never make his home, but from which, in his brief visits, he may bring a new conception of spirit and of life, be newborn to a new earth.

He thought of his mother and her rapturous delight in such scenes. He wished she might stand with him here, on one of the highest peaks in the range, and look out on the billowy expanse of peaks and canyons that broke away suddenly eastward into the flat, limitless plains of Eastern Colorado and Kansas. As though across a vast distance he saw himself, the small, sickly boy, seated beside his mother, listening to her stories of the Rockies. It was her stories that had brought him here, to the top of Long's Peak alone.

He returned home with new vision. From now on he was absorbed with the idea of taking others to the top of the Peak. First he must prepare himself thoroughly for the job. He would explore the entire region, know the canyon, lakes, and peaks around it, and be able to point out all the interesting landmarks from the top. It would take months, perhaps years, before he could master it all, but this was the field of work he was planning for himself.

His strength was still limited. There were days when he did not stir far from his cabin. But he put in the time watching the life around him. The bluebirds had nested again under the ridge log, and their companionship filled each day with delight. They raised two broods again this summer, and the young birds were to Enos a never-ending source of entertainment and study. Their helplessness surprised him, for even after they were out of the nest and as large as their parents, they would continue to coax for worms in the most pleading fashion. That they had many enemies, the weasels, stray cats and dogs in the neighborhood, Enos also learned, and was constantly on the alert to protect them.

It was a great existence, living like this, outdoors all day, sleeping in the quiet cabin, giving an hour or two a day to study, and he continued to increase in health, often going without eating for a day or two if his stomach trouble returned. His mother had been right when she said the mountains would be good for him. It would take time, he realized, to overcome the difficulty entirely, to have that assurance of health that would allow him to do the unlimited exploration he was planning. If it were not for the necessity of making a living, he would have stayed on in his cabin, which still remained unfinished. He was waiting until he could afford to add the much-needed floor without drawing out all his savings.

Enos might have gone back to the ranch where he had spent the previous winter. But he wanted to see new scenes, try his hand at a different kind of work. Perhaps he could earn more wages. The kind of work did not matter, so long as it offered opportunity to learn something new and broaden his range of activity. Butte, Montana, was being much talked of everywhere as the most wide awake center in the West, and might be his best opportunity for an all-round new and interesting experience.

He would start early so he could walk part of the way, see some of the country, as well as save train fare. It was a long way to Butte, and would be a long way back if he did not find a job. But he would make it, just as he made the Rockies. And he would accomplish his ever-increasing desire to expand his range of knowledge, his contacts with the world of action, and gain the confidence which he would need in leading people up the trail to the top of Long's Peak. And so the boy of seventeen, an undeveloped, immature boy for his age, made another leap into the unknown.

Miners at the Anaconda Copper Mine.
Enos is seated at bottom, far left.

A Miner at Butte

"To step from a great mining camp into a library is like stepping from madness to reason, from darkness to light. At one there is noise, a beating and mangling of the earth in order to tear away its golden Idol. A specimen is sacred; a stockholder a god. At the library, whosoever will may come and take specimens and nuggets galore. The only limit is capacity. Ruskin declares the veins of wealth lie within the brain. Every library is a World's Fair; it contains the masterpieces of master minds. It is an intellectual sky—glowing with planets, satellites, and stars. In this glittering realm, Shakespeare is the Sun."
    Enos A. Mills, 1897

It was an exciting experience to young Mills to find himself in the midst of life in a roaring mining town. The frantic traffic of the streets surprised and bewildered him; six-horse ore wagons mingled with smart traps and elegant victorias; there were men on horseback and delivery wagons rattling over the cobblestone pavements, burros, oxen, and mules; and even astonishing trolley cars running by electric power on narrow rails, only just coming into use.

The sidewalks were equally crowded and quite as conglomerate, and formed an index to Butte's inhabitants. Miners in their rough working clothes predominated, touching elbows with cowboys in from the range, army officers, soldiers, a sailor or two from San Francisco, Chinese with pigtails flapping, an Indian shrouded to the eyes in his blanket, and prospectors of every type—from the old timer with shaggy beard and dreamy eyes peering out under a battered slouch hat, shuffling along in high boots the color of desert dust, his nondescript clothes as much a part of him as his wrinkled skin, to the younger sons and remittance-men from England, in tweeds, swinging a cane, wearing an "old school" tie, bringing their clipped speech to mingle with the dialects from every corner of the United States.

The cries of the newsboys arrested his attention, and he bought a copy of the "Anaconda Standard", with the idea of locating a job. He might as well start at once, since that was the really important thing ahead for him. He found that a "toolboy" was wanted at the Anaconda Mine, and as soon as he could get his directions, he set off to apply.

The foreman thought he was rather small for the job, but was impressed by something about the boy that suggested he might be capable beyond his years. At any rate, he agreed to give him a trial, and told him he could come back the following day. But Enos lingered about the mine. If he was going to work there, he might as well begin to learn all he could. He saw the men changing shifts, got bits of their conversation, began to get hold of mining terms and to understand the drift of their talk. And before the day was over, he met another tool-boy, John Lloyd, who offered to take him along where he was boarding.

Lloyd liked the boy, for Enos's honesty and sincerity were as evident as his red hair and clear blue eyes. He told Enos he could share his room until he could look around and find something more to his liking. Enos plied him with questions about the mine, the duties of a tool-boy, the various terms he would need to know to work intelligently. Lloyd in turn had questions about Colorado, the mountains, the climate, the mines, and the then still young Denver City. Enos always found it easy to talk about Colorado, especially about the mountains he loved. But the talk presently drifted back to the Anaconda, its history, its phenomenal development, and the men who had made it. When the next day came he already had an intelligent introduction to the mine and the miners that served him to good purpose in handling the duties assigned him.

A tool-boy spends his time between the blacksmith's shop at the mine entrance and the men working in the drifts. Loading up with the sharpened drills, Mills dropped to the different levels, put the tools on a truck, and sped with this to the points where the men were at work. As they called for a fresh drill, chucking the dulled one on the "mutt"—debris of crushed rock—he handed it out and hurried on to the next call. Returning, he gathered up the used drills and delivered them to the smithy, reloading again with a new set for the men in the drifts. A miner would often use three or four drills in boring only a few inches of the two-to-four-foot holes. So the life of a tool-boy, or "nipper," as the miners called him, was practically one of perpetual motion.

Portrait
of Enos,
Butte,
Montana.

Mills proved a good nipper. He did his work with the wholehearted efficiency characteristic of him. It was an excellent way to become familiar with the mine. He was alert to the work going on around him, learned much about drilling and timbering from observation and asking questions. Just to know his own work was not enough. He might not make mining his profession, but, at any rate, he would acquire all the knowledge he could about it.

He liked the men with whom he came in contact; their ruggedness, their independence appealed to him. Their life work had been mining. Mostly men a good deal older than he, among them hardrock miners from Cornwall speaking an odd dialect in singing voices; Irish, too, lively and quarrelsome, ready with a joke and impatient at being kept waiting a

Enos with two
Butte, Montana
friends:
At left: Tim Lynch;
John Lloyd on right.
Circa 1900.

moment for a sharpened drill; American from pretty much every section of the country. Fine workers all, and proud of their craft. Enos was interested in their talk of other lands—England, Bohemia, Germany, and faraway places, and their different experiences at Cripple Creek, in Utah, California, New Mexico, and Arizona.

At that time, the winter of 1887-88, Butte was a lively, hustling, prosperous city of between ten and fifteen thousand persons, a third or more of the population being employed in the mines, generally at high wages. Surrounded by pine clad mountains, whose peaks carried snow winter and summer, the climate was consistently exhilarating, befitting the adventurous spirit of the inhabitants and stimulating their natural activities. Butte, in fact, was busy in a hundred ways, growing fast, working and playing hard, and reaching out for whatever the world could give it in return for the gold, silver, and copper it was producing in unbelievable quantities. Enos reacted to the spirit of the place, and was accepted at his own, true worth.

Though the main thought of those in Butte was the mineral wealth of the region, there were plenty of social and intellectual activities. There were good schools, churches, several newspapers, and a fine library. The last was to be a goldmine to Enos. Lloyd introduced him to its shelves early in their acquaintance, and Enos lost no time in taking out a card.

From then on, as Lloyd later related, "Enos sat up half the night reading and writing." He had never before had access to a library, and it is probable that he hardly knew where to being to explore in this wealth of fact, fiction, travel, science, philosophy and poetry. It is certain that he read much of Burns and Shakespeare. Always fond of poetry, he familiarized himself with the best, and collected scrapbooks of favorite quotations and selections that appealed to him in his wide reading.

In his constant use of the library he came in contact with some of the members of the University Club. He was invited to their gatherings and began to aspire to literary efforts of his own. In November of this year 1887, he read a poem, "Among the Rockies," which appears to be of his own composition, before the University Club. While not remarkable as verse, the swing and color of the lines reveal the boy's enthusiasm for Nature as well as the dawning urge to express himself in writing. A few other evidences of this poetry writing day remain, but it is doubtful if much of it ever reached the public.

Whenever opportunity afforded, Enos and Lloyd went tramping in these "Grand Montana Mountains," of which he said:

> "Thy rocky heights and crystals,
>   Thy sparkling waters sing,
> And intermingling echoes
>   From cliffs to gorges ring."

Before spring reached summer, soon after his eighteenth birthday, he won his promotion from tool-boy to miner. He had every reason to be satisfied with his winter at Butte. He had set aside a neat sum in the bank and he had made many friends. He had widened his horizon and gained a bigger conception of life. But the longing for his mountain valley became intense. He wanted to be up on Long's Peak again, to wander all over it, and to be back in the seclusion of his cabin. It was better to leave Butte for the summer, for the underground work had not improved his health, and the attacks of indigestion persisted.

"I'll be back in the fall," he told Lloyd in leaving, "but it will be good to get back to Colorado for a while. I like Butte, and I like mining, but what I want most is to be a guide, the best guide in the Rocky Mountains."

It was early June when Enos reached home and spring was well advanced. Quite different, he recalled, from the preceding year when he had watched each sign of spring's slow coming; had seen the aspens bud into catkins, then spread their tiny green leaves; had enjoyed the returning birds in their happy deliberation of house hunting and nest building, intermingled with bursts of song; and had marveled over the procession of bloom that filled the meadows with a riot of color.

But even if he had not been home to welcome the bluebirds when they returned, at least they had not forgotten the protection they had enjoyed the two preceding summers. Again they were nesting under the ridge log! They flew to meet him as he slowly approached the cabin, fluttering over his head, resting on his arm briefly, while he spoke to them in gentle tones. It was a glad homecoming, happier because he would again have the companionship of the bird family over his doorway.

Enos put in a few days around his cabin, walking among his trees, noting the homes of other birds, stopping to let rabbits hop by unfrightened, filling his eyes with the grandeur of Long's Peak and the long sweep of the fresh, green valley. He strolled down the beaver stream, saw baby beaver taking an exciting swim, caught a fleeting glimpse of deer in the distance, knew there were probably young ones hidden nearby. Each new interest drew him toward it; his eyes took in more than his mind could do justice to.

This summer his was to specialize, he was to devote his thought to guiding. It was not enough to know the trail, the direction to go; he must be able to act in emergencies, must know when and how to help other climbers, and to set a pace which all could easily follow to the top. Enos took advantage of every opportunity to go with other climbers that summer, not as a guide, but for the experience of seeing how they made the trip. Almost invariably he found they rushed the trail instead of using their strength deliberately, thus not only missing much of the beauty along the way, but reaching the top exhausted from misspent energies, if they reached it at all.

He laid out a strenuous program for himself and eventually accomplished it. He climbed the Peak alone time after time. He went up on clear, calm days, by moonlight, and then in darkest night. He climbed when the top was wreathed in clouds, and again when the wind seemed determined to push him off; he lingered in thunderstorms to see where lightning struck and to watch the electrical effects around him. He learned to know the weather under any and all conditions, and discovered that the tops of high peaks are most often in sunshine, serene above cloud and storm.

When Enos was satisfied that he could find the trail under the worst conditions, endurance tests were made. One of these consisted in making a quick round trip, then, after only a few minutes' rest, shouldering thirty pounds of supplies and hastening to the rescue of an imaginary climber ill on the summit. Several trips were made simply to learn the swiftest pace he could maintain from bottom to summit without a rest. This proved especially valuable to him, for no matter what pace others set, he held to an even, deliberate rate of speed as best in its results.

One of the interesting visitors to the Park this summer was Frederick H. Chapin, of the Appalachian Mountain Club. He had visited the region the two preceding summers, and had become greatly interested in the icecaps that fringed the eastern edge of the higher peaks. These had been little studied; in fact, with the exception of the work done by the Hayden Geological Survey of 1871, there had been no extensive explorations in the Park. Enos had an opportunity to join in some of Chapin's glacier studying expeditions, and had a new insight into the movement and workings of glaciers. The winters of 1886 to 1888 had been particularly snowless, and the glaciers revealed their crevasses, grooved surfaces, and formations to good advantage. These miniature glaciers, numerous and varied remnants of the Ice Age, were glimpses into another world and opened up a new field of study for Enos.

Chapin explored many then unknown and even unnamed peaks. He probably added many names to the scenes photographed, Ypsilon Peak, Hallett's Peak, and Hallett's Glacier, although the latter name has recently been changed to Rowe Glacier in honor of its discoverer, Israel Rowe, a pioneer hunter of 1876.

Estes Park had far-flung boundaries; it extended from the canyon entrances to the top of the Divide, and reached out into all the semi-enclosed smaller parks along the Big Thompson and Fall Rivers and their tributaries. Settlers were not slow in finding the more desirable locations of Moraine, Horseshoe, Beaver, and Bartholf Parks, the North End, and the more open Fish Creek and Mary's Lake country. The straggling summer population camped along the trout-filled streams or found adequate accommodations with the year round residents: at Elkhorn Lodge, run by Mr. And Mrs. W. E. James; at the Estes Park Hotel, built by Lord Dunraven; at Ferguson's Ranch, known as "The Highlands"; and Sprague's Ranch, in what was then Moraine Park; or at Lamb's guiding headquarters, later to be known as "The Long's Peak House." There was no effort made to advertise the region, and for the fifteen years between 1877 and 1892 it simply existed.

The higher slopes above nine thousand feet were utter wildness, a region of rugged, forested canyons, glaciers, alpine lakes, high grassy plateaus, and rocky peaks. These magnificent scenes were almost unknown to the outside world, and even to the people living within comparatively easy reach of them. There were few trails, except those made by game and followed by hunters. Wild life was plentiful. Black and grizzly bear "infested" the canyons. A numerous mountain sheep population ranged the higher slopes unmolested. Deer and elk roamed at large over the more open meadows, and grouse were common. Foxes, lynx, and coyotes prowled at will, and mountain lions occasionally ventured down into the settlements for tame mutton. Here was sport, scenery, and seclusion for everyone.

The beauty of this broken, mountainous realm was made more enchanting by numerous sparkling streams, dashing down from the heights and watering the fertile valleys. The dense growths of forest were delightfully varied with Engelmann and Douglas spruce, lodgepole, limber, and western yellow pine, balsam fir, and the bright quaking aspen. For its thousand varieties of wild flowers alone, the region might well have become famous, the succession of bloom in the different elevations prolonging the flower season through out the summer. Every alpine meadow was a richly tinted wildflower garden, while looking down from the summit of Long's Peak, one season, Enos states, "so closely and completely do some varieties crowd and color that entire slopes glow red with rattleweed or spread white masses of snowy mariposa lilies, though fifteen miles from the summit—one of the most gorgeous robings in which Nature has ever wrapped herself for the reward of her worshipers."

But the worshipers of Nature were few. It is probable that not more than a dozen parties found their way to the top of Long's Peak each summer. Isabella Bird's interesting volume, "A Lady's Life in the Rocky Mountains" had appeared in 1879 and created a sensation in the mountaineering world. Her descriptions of the scenes around Estes Park and her thrilling experiences in climbing Long's Peak in 1873 gave increased interest to travel in that direction. The difficulties in reaching the scenes did not appeal to a large number of people. The trip from the Eastern cities was made by train to Lyons, a twenty-mile stage ride to Estes Park, and then another day's excursion by horseback and afoot to the more interesting points of attraction. Except by those who had weeks of leisure to explore the uncharted canyons and peaks, the region was almost untouched. There were no guides worthy of the name; that is, none familiar with more than the one small isolated section of the Park in which he lived.

Such, in brief, was the development of Estes Park up to 1888. It was one thing to train and equip oneself for guiding, to explore this vast territory of broken, rugged topography and feel at home in it anywhere; and quite another and seemingly still more difficult undertaking to bring people in contact with it. It would not be accomplished in a year or in several years, perhaps, but the possibilities with the region offered in such abundant measure for attracting greater numbers of people strongly impressed Enos as worth developing.

One immediate need was a better trail up Long's Peak. Carlyle Lamb was persuaded to undertake this project with him. A trail was laid out from Lamb's Ranch, somewhat along the general direction of the present one below timberline. It would be shorter than the then used trail across the slope of Estes Cone, and easier for horses. It was agreeable work in a measure to Enos, with the soft winds playing in the pines and setting the aspen leaves aflutter, and touched with visions of the procession of climbers who in time would come to follow it into the wilderness.

The summer went all too swiftly, with trail trips, trail work, and further completion of his cabin. The region was becoming more and more a part of him, and he a part of it. He was still developing, physically and mentally, growing up to the serious future that stretched, far, far ahead. The world looked good to him; spending some months in his cabin each year, with the knowledge of a well paid job in prospect, gave him plenty of action and opportunity for study and advancement. Though guiding was his chosen profession, in the winter he went back to mining.

It was good to meet old friends again, and they welcomed him back to the mine. He assumed his new duties with the same painstaking thoroughness that had advanced him from nipper to miner in so short a time. The hardrock miner's craft takes plenty of study and a good miner has a right to be proud. There were Cornishmen at the Anaconda who had been at work for twenty-five years, and who would answer, to some stranger's question, "Are you a miner?" "Me? Say, I've been drilling rock these many years, but a miner, now, that takes some doing." But let another make the same statement in regard to his ability and he would probably get his head punched.

Mills watched the best men at work when off shift himself, asked questions about anything that was new to him, took all the advice these men could give. Now and then one of the men who appreciated his earnestness allowed him to work a drill, explained the method of the work, the position of the holes into which the powder was to be crammed. The powder-monkey, as the carrier of the dangerous stuff was called, was usually an older man, fit for his responsibility. He had not only to bring the powder, but to keep it fit to use, just warm enough to be soft. Mills would stop when not too pressed to watch the charges rammed home.

Enos was in good physical condition when he returned to Butte, the outdoor life and exercise of the summer had been beneficial. He determined to get more exercise than the work in the mine provided. Indian clubs and dumbbells were employed faithfully each day, not only to keep his muscles in form, but to keep the red blood circulating through his brain and body. He wanted a clear head for his work and for the intense reading which he had mapped out for himself.

He discovered Dickens, Thackeray, Macaulay, Washington Irving, Parkman, Stevenson, Scott, all the classics and very much history and travel. And he was exploring further into knowledge and literature, was mastering the work of Huxley, Tyndall, Wallace, Darwin, Spencer, Paine, and Ingersoll, who in that day were revolutionizing thought. Deep thought for a boy of eighteen! The library was probably the best in the West; it was patronized by readers who demanded this. For Butte was such an open forum for progressive thought and free speech. The red-hot political discussion turned Enos's attention to governmental history and political economy. He was already forming his opinions, as the following quotation in an old notebook would suggest:

"If wealth was not so congested, if the masses received their due, they would be empowered and would purchase extensively. If all consumers purchased only enough to give themselves civilized comforts the quantity used by them would be enormous. Protectionists overlook this. Monopolies destroy the commerce, the comforts and virtues of the people."

The last sentence, especially, he was to find opportunity many years later to voice more publicly.

That he was not hesitant in expressing his opinions even then was evidenced in an open debate with a Catholic priest on "Evolution." He collected a vast amount of material on the subject, and in some of his notes are extracts which doubtless colored his entire life and study.

"In science the first condition of success is an honest receptivity and a willingness to abandon all preconceived opinions, however cherished, if they be found to contradict the truth." Tyndall.

"Plants are the thermometers of the ages by which climatic extremes and climates in general are best measured." Gray.

"Evolution is the name of a branch of science; it is a theory of organic existence; it is a method of investigation; and it is the basis of a system of philosophy." Jordan.

One of his most fortunate chance acquaintances at Butte was a New York doctor, for whom he had done some slight service. The doctor in return, realizing the boy's none too rugged constitution, asked if he could be of service. Enos diagnosed his trouble as best he could and immediately received the unusual prescription:

"It is probably that you are unable to digest starchy foods and they should be entirely eliminated from your diet. But as a quicker remedy I would suggest you go on a complete fast for ten days. Drink all the water you want, nothing else. You won't starve in this length of time and it will enable your system to eliminate the poison. Drop in and see me every day or two, and if there is any reason to vary my instructions I'll tell you."

"Will I have to go to bed, give up work?" was Enos's only reply. He did not hesitate to follow the doctor's instructions. They seemed logical to him, but he did not want to miss a day in the mine unless necessary.

"Certainly not," the doctor answered. "Exercise in moderation will speed up the work."

When Enos did not appear at mealtime everyone was alarmed.

"No, nothing wrong, just fasting," Enos explained.

Lloyd was worried. Dieting was a new idea to most people at that time, and fasting unheard of by these hearty miners. But he said nothing to Enos, for he felt sure the boy had given his usual serious consideration to the proposition. It was with relief, however, that he observed the fast to have no injurious effects.

In fact, at the end of the ten day fast Enos joined in a game of baseball with no more effort or exertion than the rest of the team. Everyone proclaimed him a wonder.

To Enos the wonderful part was that he began to feel better, and on the starchless diet which the doctor had prescribed he continued to improve. While he had often tried to work out a diet of his own, even fasting a day or two when at his worst, he now made a study of the subject, and with the doctor's help got started on the road too good health. Of course, he couldn't expect a miracle, to have a lifelong trouble cured in a day, but by carefully systematizing his eating, he built up an endurance for continued effort and physical hardships that enabled him to accomplish much-desired ends.

Enos's reputation for going against established customs brought about much jollying from his companions, which he took good-naturedly and enjoyed. In fact, Pat Harrington was known to be constantly on the watch to have an excuse to call attention to some new departure from the ordinary.

One day the men were changing into work clothes in the shed when Pat had his own surprise. Enos had just invested in a novel brand of underwear just being advertised.

"What's them things?" Pat asked, by way of provoking a laugh from his companions.

"Don't you see, I've joined the Union," Enos answered, and the laugh was on Pat. Debate for and against the Union being at the time a burning issue.

The life at Butte was full of contrasts. Although the miners worked on Sunday, they could, if they chose, visit the saloons, go to the opera, attend church, or spend time in the public library. The mines were almost as busy at night as during daylight, and "Whatley's Cafe," always open, was sure to be crowded at one o'clock in the morning. But Butte was orderly. As Enos wrote: "Butte has no 'bad men.' They were laid to rest with boots on several years ago. The police have only common experiences and the sheriff might be easily mistaken for a visiting drummer. Like all mining towns, it is saturated with saloons and charged with chance. Big purses have led some of the best horses in the world to the Butte Racecourse and one lively day the betting public passed one million dollars through the pool boxes. Butte is world known for spirited receptions to prominent visitors and the crowd that greeted one lecturer was so large he thought he saw everyone in Butte. The city is ever ready to honor genius, reward talent or welcome merit. A popular Opera House manager once received a $10,000 benefit. The many thousand dollars required for one reception were easily raised by donations in a few hours' soliciting, Marcus Daily and Senator Clark heading the list of subscribers with $2500 each."

An incident which occurred a number of years later well illustrates Enos's independent spirit, as well as the influences under which it grew in the progressive town of Butte.

On the outbreak of a smallpox epidemic the city passed an ordinance compelling vaccinations. Enos refused to be vaccinated. He contended that good health, cleanliness, and public sanitation alone prevented smallpox. He quoted Alfred Russel Wallace's opinion that vaccination was one of the six great errors of humanity during the nineteenth century. He also said, "I do not question the motives of doctors who vaccinate or the sincerity of anyone who advocates vaccination, but if vaccination prevents smallpox, those who are vaccinated have nothing to fear from those who are not." His convictions were such that he offered to go to the pest-house and rub his hands on any inmate there. And did. His health was at the best by this time and he had no fear of the disease, while the evil consequences of vaccination, in some cases, had been impressed upon him. He did not contract smallpox. The agitation against compulsory vaccination was so intense that the ordinance was revoked for a period.

Enos spent much of the following years at Butte. He was always sure of good wages and his advancement in the mine continued. Before he was twenty-one he was made night foreman. He rose from the inexperienced nipper to miner, machine-driller, compressor-man, and finally to stationary engineer. The life was full of action, the thought of the day was progressive, and he developed in every way. The profession of mining was one of great possibilities, but did not afford, to him, the opportunity for greatest development. The phenomenal influences of Nature made the stronger appeal, and whenever he acquired a bank reserve he abandoned the mining for weeks and months of camping and exploring that were to prepare him for his greater field of usefulness and to enrich his life.

New Conceptions of Life

"Sometime the grizzled prospector will lead his stubborn burro down the mountain and cease the search for gold, sometime the miner will lay down his pick, blow out his candle and leave the empty mine, sometime eternal night will come upon the gas and the coal-oil lamp. But our gardens of wild beauty are immortal. They will give us their inspiration forever."

Enos A. Mills

It was a beautiful Spring, May, 1889, when Enos returned to Estes Park, and he leaped out of the stage in high spirits. The coming of the twice-a-week stage always brought out the general population for miles around, eager for the news of the outside world as well as the incidental purpose of neighborly visiting: Sprague and Ferguson swapping stories on weather wisdom; Jones and Hupp eager to get their daily papers and return to Beaver Park before nightfall; James, McGregor, Lester, Husted, and others discussing the prospect of an early summer, and Cleave, the postmaster, occupied with his mail bags.

"Well, how's old Montana?" they greeted Enos. "Pure gold by now, likely."

"Say, didn't you know 'Copper is King'!" he exclaimed loyally.

They were interested in his stories of Butte; news from a mining town was always exciting.

"Can't understand why you don't stay there," one remarked; "nothing'd suit me better than to have a chance to try mining once."

"Yes, it's a great life," Enos agreed, "but I have to get back to my homestead before the packrats carry it off," a mountain allusion which always provoked mirth.

"Say, now, what you got up there but a bunch of rocks? And they're probably snowed in yet. Never could see why you want to live way up there in that lonesome valley."

"It's the best place on earth to live. Why don't you come up sometime? I'll show you Long's Peak. Planning to guide this summer, and we're going to have a good trail, too; lots more people'll be climbing it from now on."

"Well, they can, if they want; plum foolish, I say, with all this scenery close by to waste their energy on. No, sir, I ain't lost nothing on top of Long's yet. It must have a heap of snow on it still, judging by what's lying back in the timber. Some weeks before you'll be able to get up there, I imagine."

That was just what Enos wanted to find out—how much snow there was on the trail and on top, and whether he could climb it yet with safety. But he did not pursue the subject. "The Peak had gone to his head," they would probably say.

Enos shouldered his pack and started homeward. He never lingered long in the village; his mind did not seem to run in the same track as others', his ideas always struck them as queer—wanting to do things no one else seemed interested in, content to live alone in his cabin, often without seeing another person for weeks at a stretch.

It was a wonderful mountain day, the air full of sparkle, and the late afternoon sun already sending long shadows of the pines across the quiet, restful landscape. Enos went leisurely, enjoying the profusion of flowers, wild iris, buttercups, fragrant candytuft, and bright blue mertensia, intermingling their beauty. Before him rose the gently lifting country, the nearer forested hills and ridges massed against the snowy peaks of the Divide. Long's Peak, toward which Enos walked, towered serenely above them. The meandering wagon road climbed around the base of Prospect Mountain, past Ferguson's Ranch, "The Highlands," and skirted the shore of Mary's Lake. Enos rested his pack while he watched the group of mountain sheep that were frequently to be seen in the region, attracted by the alkaline deposits around the lake. The proud ram was quick to detect him, but unafraid the sheep grazed leisurely in the fresh spring pastures. Enos was in no hurry now, though eager to reach his cabin, and knowing full well the suddenness with which daylight fades in the mountains. Long he watched this wildlife drama, studying each individual character as he approached step by step, slowly, nearer and nearer. The sentinel alone appeared to observe him, but without a flicker of fear or excitement. Then, retreating with the same deliberate movements, he left the sheep in the same peaceful content he had found them.

Onward through the gathering darkness, Enos climbed the shoulder of Lily Mountain and paused at Lily Lake to get the last bit of sunset glory, glittering on the Mummy Range and reflected in the water. He must linger, too, by the beaver house and view the ever interesting canals the beaver had made so extensively the preceding fall to bring down their food supply from the aspen up the hillside. Every mile of the homeward journey was filled with interest, old or new. The stars were shining brightly as he climbed up through the dense lodgepole forest over the gentle divide between Estes Cone and Twin Sisters, and down into his own Long's Peak Valley, the first settler to return that season.

The music of mountain streams, resounding pleasantly in the distance, mingled with the gentle rustle of pine needles and the occasional call of the nighthawk or the Wilson's snipe. His steps quickened as the distance between him and his cabin grew shorter, until, with a heart pounding with happiness, he distinguished the meager outline of his home.

He lingered in the doorway, hoping to get a sound from the nest beneath the ridge log, but all was quiet. A lamp was lit, an eager survey made of the simple interior to assure him that all was as he left it, and he relaxed into the natural, tired boy that he was, released from exacting labors and civilized conventions again, and went to bed. The sweet night air slipped in through the open doorway, an owl hooted in the distance, the stars twinkled through the darkness, a coyote called across the valley—but whether it was answered or not Enos never knew.

There was a fluttering of wings outside the cabin, the daylight was just breaking, Enos was awake, wide awake. Moving quietly to the doorway, he was greeted by a pair of bluebirds—his bluebirds. They were not alarmed by his presence, in fact they seemed to be expecting it, poised in the air on fluttering wings over his head, as though trying to show their welcome. All day, as they were flying back and forth carrying nesting material, they frequently paused to circle around him, or rested momentarily on the pole fence beside him as he watched their busy activities. When he went into the cabin they followed, seemingly asking him to stay near, within sight of them. But soon the nest was completed and Mrs. Bluebird settled down to domestic duties with her bright mate watching from the nearby fence.

Enos put in every day in self-directed preparation for guiding. His winter's study had advanced his knowledge in many directions and his tramps up and down the mountain were filled with a better understanding of its geology and natural history. Still vague, his knowledge, but growing; he was applying the general principles which he had learned to the particulars he saw. Constantly seeking for cause and effect, he was storing away in his mind observations that were to serve him to good purpose; and also many unexplained phases of Nature which would require further study. Always, as he worked on the trail or followed it to the top of the Peak, his quick, clear glance registered the life of the wilderness about him; what he saw he remembered, and he saw so much more than most, loving wild Nature as he did. The mountains were not simply huge elevations of the earth's surface up which one climbed laboriously to get a view or make a climbing record; the forests, the valleys, the streams and lakes were not merely places in which to hunt, trap or fish, to camp in or ride through blindly. The big outdoors was a natural Universe whose every detail was of absorbing interest and beauty, an inexhaustible field for study, refreshing to the mind no less than to the body, more precious, more vital in what it had to teach than all the universities in the land. Books were useful, necessary, but one must take them to Nature to be interpreted.

May passed. June came with occasional tourists, putting up at Lamb's or camping out among the pine and aspen in the valley. One day an opportunity came for Enos to take a party up Long's Peak, inexperienced climbers whom Carlyle didn't think could make the top. But Enos was willing to undertake the job of getting them there, or at least to take them as far as they were able to go. Like many other would-be climbers, they felt they were good walkers and would make the trip easily. They wasted their breath in talking and their time in frequent resting. Enos discovered that it would be necessary for the guide to do the talking in the future. It was a long day and a full one, for though the party had never been on a mountain before, they were sure they knew more about Long's Peak than the guide; that is, on the way up they took occasion to assert their own judgement; coming home they were not so sure of themselves, though much wiser. It was evident to Enos from this experience that the guide must be the dictator. Though he had learned the Peak from bottom to top, and from top to bottom, he still had much to learn about human nature.

Returning to his cabin after dark, he realized there had been a tragedy in the bluebird nest. Five speckle-bibbed baby birds were calling for food and the mother's warmth that had protected them. Carrying the nest and its five hungry orphans into his cabin, he proceeded to warm their shivering bodies and to plan how he could bring them up.

The parent birds that had learned to trust man had been betrayed. A small boy with a gun from a neighboring tourist camp, new to the wilds and the ways of bird life, had thought it great fun to return with his trophies.

For Enos the tragedy was not only a personal loss, but brought new and time-consuming responsibility. From dawn till dark he labored to provide food, the right kind and enough of it, for his adopted bird family. One had died the first day, and another met an accident a little later, but the other three thrived on the fare provided and furnished enough amusement and entertainment to repay him fully for the responsibility assumed. His close observations of bluebird ways the three preceding summers had made it possible for him to provide the essentials, though there were doubtless many innovations in the training of these youngsters. The bluebirds came to depend on him for everything, and there is no knowing how deeply the experience influenced and colored his life. He says, "I had planned simply to enjoy seeing the parents feed and train these children for their brief and busy existence. Then came the sad event that changed the even tenor of passing days and asked me to be far more than I had ever been and different than I had ever dreamed of being."

This most unusual of bird experiences is told in "Bird Memories of the Rockies" under the title "The Love Song of Little Blue," and gives a special insight into the richness of Mills's character and the subtle influences that Nature threw around him in his youth.

Realizing that the little birds might become too dependent on him, Enos often turned to his studying and reading, devoting an hour or two a day to grammar and writing. He had added to his bookshelf and reading much about the early explorers and adventurers who had blazed trails into the unknown West. Out of his reading and thinking he compiled articles of his own on the Lewis and Clark Expedition, thrilled with the fact that they had led their party successfully without a single death, with the one exception of a member who had been ill at the start. It was to him an illustrious example of what guides should be. He had also become greatly interested in the civilization of the Incas, and gathered an enormous array of facts about Peru. He assimilated his material and compiled an eleven-thousand-word article on the subject.

"Little Blue," as his favorite of the three little birds came to be called, would often become restless and clamor for attention. If Enos was too absorbed to leave his writing, "Little Blue" would perch on the table, following the slow movement of the pen, and listening to the story Enos read to him.

The little birds stayed around the cabin all summer, demanding his thought and attention, if not his entire time. But he probably profited most from the experience. He frequently urged others to follow a definite nature interest, saying, "An acquaintance with a single bird, animal, or flower develops the sympathies and promotes universal brotherhood." Surely he could speak from experience. The summer had been one of the richest in his life.

September was made lonely by the flight of the bluebirds for the Southland, but Enos lingered on, trailing the heights and spending days along timberline. Here he saw many of the migratory birds, resting on their long flight and picnicking on the season's latest berries and fruits. Here summer made its last stand; here the old, storm-beaten trees maintained their steadfast hold against the seasons. It was a time of year which he loved best. He ends his "Story of Estes Park and a Guide Book" with the following prose and poetry:

"Fortunate is the visitor who can linger into autumn. In September the grass comes out in tan, the willows in red, while the maples burst into flame and the aspens change to pure gold. Everywhere is rich repose. The hours are clear and calm, and in the golden peace of the autumn days the flowers fade one by one.

"In the mellow haze of the Autumn days,
  With the aspen's golden rhyme;
With many a sigh I say good-bye
  To the good old Summer time."

There was many a night when he lighted his oil lamp and read till midnight, in the grip for his passion for improvement, for progress. "Fourteen Weeks in Natural Philosophy" (J. Dorman Steele) was mastered. He was constantly studying history, writing out his own compositions on "Egypt," "Greece," "Siberia," and "Mexico," as well as on "Kansas" and "Arizona." And biography interested him. He was inspired by the independent, helpful lives of Elizabeth Cady Stanton, Thomas Jefferson, David Crockett, and Abraham Lincoln; of whom he writes, "Was very ambitious through life but found plenty of time to be honest, generous and kind." Of William Lloyd Garrison he notes: "Inherited his better qualities from a kind and intelligent mother. He also inherited a princely share of poverty...He did not care for show, flattery, or applause, yet it must have been a source of satisfaction to him in his old age to be pointed out to children 'as the good man who had the courage to begin the glorious work for freedom years ago.' It requires the greatest courage to battle against popular opinion without hope of reward, and bravery to do duty in the face of danger without flinching; so I think he is one of the noblest of heroes."

He labored with penmanship and spelling as well as the ability to express himself. Self-imposed tasks, without the encouragement of teachers, and carried through regardless of the lack of impelling examinations and tests. Where interest is the taskmaster, there is true brain development. As he has occasion to say in "Children of my Trail School" ("Adventures of a Nature Guide"): "In human psychology it is ever important to get results while working under morale, using all the power that interest adds. Thus finally you accomplish the most difficult and greatest results through the supreme, sustained efforts that desire and interest make possible. Natural phenomena interest and stimulate the mind in a thousand ways."

His time was his own and he used it to constant purpose. Many days and nights were spent along the beaver stream, and exploring the colonies farther from home. He was constantly forming opinions about beaver work and beaver characteristics which later discoveries proved incorrect. This never discouraged him. It was the greatest corrective possible to compare his observations in one colony with similar features in another. He soon realized that no two dams were alike; that the tree cutting varied not only in different colonies, but with different beaver; that the amount of food gathered for winter depended on the number in the colony, or upon the available food supply, or favorable or unfavorable conditions of weather and the handicap of preying enemies.

While watching in beaver colonies, stretched out behind a boulder or in a convenient treetop, he constantly saw other life for which he was not looking. Bears often walked into the scene, turning over anthills or digging out a fat chipmunk; bobcats and coyotes prowled around the ponds hoping to catch a beaver off guard; squirrels scampered busily up and down tree trunks, cutting and gathering cones with the precious ripened nuts for winter; everywhere there was a show going on in this big, outdoor museum.

At this time it was possible to watch beaver working in the daytime, in secluded regions where they had not been molested by man. His opportunities for beaver study were unusual. Even in later years he never ceased to devote much of his time each autumn to beaver activities, even though this required nights of close and difficult observation. By daily visits he checked up on the work of the night before, and kept accurate records of the changes through the years. Old colonies were occasionally abandoned; trees sprouted and grew again and the ponds filled with sediment. Eventually the beaver might return.

Autumn slipped gradually into winter. There were days and nights when the wind boomed in the forest above his cabin like the waves breaking on a rocky coastline; it whirled the snow in spiral columns or sent it marching in solid masses along the western horizon. Then would come days of calm, with moderate temperature and bright blue skies. The snow in the valley would quickly vanish, deer and sheep grazed around, blue jays and gray jays came out of the woods to his feeding table, with the cheerful chickadees. The woodpile must be frequently replenished, water carried from the spring, a little cooking accomplished each day; but Enos early learned how to simplify his scheme of things, to eliminate the non-essentials. There were occasional trips to Estes Park for mail and provisions, where he sometimes lingered a day or two, exploring in other directions. His interest was not confined to his own immediate environment; he saw the mountains as a whole, each section adding interest to the other, in their variety, their similarities and their contrasts. The changes in the vegetation and life at different elevations was feature that early appealed to him. He has strikingly portrayed this phase of the mountains in "Life Zones" in "Rocky Mountain National Park."

Letters came from John Lloyd during the months he was in his cabin, with alluring news of the mining activities and the rapidly developing Butte City. Enos had hopes of seeing more of the Northwest, too, and few months at work again would be good for his bank account. So, closing up his cabin for the winter, he was off to mining for the third season.

As he turned his steps northward, he thought of the little bluebirds on their journey to southern lands, and wished he might see them and their comrades in the ever-changing scenes. It had been a summer of rich associations and deep emotions, and was to leave a lasting imprint on his life. The little cabin had become doubly dear to him, and he wondered if it would again welcome bluebirds. Yes, he felt confident "Little Blue" would return with a mate, recalling with happiness the touching farewell, when the bird had turned in his southbound flight to circle once more his friend and protector.

Years of Adventuring

"Play is the nearest approach to the magic fountain of youth. The wilderness still is the supreme place to rest and play. It is doubtful if any other influence is so generally and lastingly beneficial as our primeval beauty, where people and Nature ever are young."
Enos A. Mills

A calamitous fire in the Anaconda Mine, a few weeks after Enos returned, became the one absorbing interest and subject of discussion. It introduced a new factor into the scene, new conditions to be met and overcome. There was much speculation as to the cause of the fire, and, more important, as to whether work could ever be resumed again. Many miners were thrown out of work, and went to other scenes of activity. And those who remained found time heavy on their hands, life dragged. To Enos, the methods being used to quench the fire were of the greatest interest. He made extensive notes, while watching the underground conflagration; helped in the resuscitation of miners brought to the surface, overcome with gas and sulphurous fumes, and witnessed strange scenes within and around the mine. Of the methods to combat the fire, he says:

"All entrances to the mine were at once closed with the hope that the fire would be smothered, but it was not even checked. The lead was very wide, in places more than a hundred feet, and timbered with square sets which, together with the logging and bulkheads, contained enough lumber to build a city. Unable to smother the fire, fourteen boilers were put to work to force steam into the mine for two months. This took most of the enthusiasm out of the fire and work in the mine was resumed. But the fire soon assumed desperate proportions, and so hot did it become that the ore, which contained a quantity of sulphur, took fire. Gas pervaded the mine and the heat became so intense that all regular work was stopped and the drifts leading to the air shafts and adjoining mine were bulkheaded and the Anaconda filled with water to the two-hundred-foot level, the fire being on the six-hundred level. The water was pumped out and work resumed. It was then found that the fire had burned above the four-hundred-foot level and, despite bad treatment, was soon raging again. The vein seemed pleased to glow again with youthful fire. It seemed as though the fire burned better after the application of water. A stream directed at a red-hot wall of rock for an hour will cause only a little thin crust to form outside the fire, so within a few minutes after the water has ceased, the rock is glowing again. But the most successful method was to run several diamond-drill holes down to the fire and then set water flowing through the holes. The walls are cracked and blistered, adorned with copper stalactites, while underfoot rocks and cinders are cemented together with recently cooled copper."

Even the excitement of fire fighting palled after a time, and he decided to journey off to San Francisco, and to see something of that California of whose varied scenes and attractions much news had been drifting into Butte.

Enos found accommodations on Post Street, and lost no time in finding his way to the Pacific, he who had never seen the Sea, away from the city with all its varied and novel sights—it was not for these that he had come. Cities were all alike, he said; it was only the ever-changing panorama of the open, untamed spaces that held exhibits worth while. He was not disappointed in the rocky, broken coastline, the sandy beach with its lively assortment of bird life—seagulls, pelicans, cormorants—wheeling in the air, swimming the sea, or walking ungainly about; sea lions, leaping and plunging in the breakers or scrambling up on the rocks to sun themselves. It was all new and fascinating, and the beach became his favorite walk.

In one of his strolls by the ocean he stopped to examine a bit of ground-creeper, a plant with a delicious fragrance, wondering about it and how it came to grow there. There was another walker on that lonely beach, a handsome, tall, bearded man of about fifty, who approached him in friendly greeting.

The man was John Muir, and observing Enos's interest in the plant, he proceeded to tell something of its manner of growth, describing its tenacity in rooting itself more deeply as the wind removed the sand, compelling it to grow taller and put out roots higher up as the sand drifted over and covered it. It did yeoman's duty in holding down the sand, Muir added, practically. And when Enos's questions continued, he told him its scientific and popular name.

"It is one of the yuccas; we call it by its Spanish name, yerba buena, 'good herb.' The Spanish used it for infusions that were supposed to cure colds and other ailments."

And then, impressed by the young man's enthusiasm and appreciation for the information received, Muir invited him for a four mile walk across the sand hills and through the beginnings of Golden Gate Park to the end of the car line. They talked of plants and trees, of their adventures on mountain and seashore. And when they parted, Muir asked him to continue the acquaintance at his home.

There could have been no more fortunate introduction to California than this chance meeting with John Muir. Since the last of the sixties and on through the seventies, Muir had been tramping the Sierras of California, writing of the mountains, trying to awaken public interest in them. This very year he was to make an extended tour, with Robert Underwood Johnson, editor of the "Century Magazine," through Yosemite and the Big Trees. Muir was desperately anxious to bring about legislation for creating a national park in that region. So far, he had fought in vain against apathy in California, but his Scotch tenacity was not to be discouraged; he would send his message across the nation.

Enos was not long in taking advantage of Muir's invitation, and his call was the beginning of a lifelong friendship. Muir, while finishing the signing of some letters, suggested to Mills that he might glance over his library. It represented the best of its kind in print: books on geology, natural history, travel and exploration in all the far and near parts of the world. And then he talked, and there was not a more fascinating talker than John Muir on the subjects dear to him. He spoke that perfect, flowing English that so fills his books, and through the words shone his enthusiasm, the spirit of the man. Mills was one of the best listeners, and on that day he listened for the first time to a master in the very field he loved best. "Climb the mountains and get their glad tidings" was not new to Mills, but the number of exciting places in which those tidings could be heard, as Muir described them, was a revelation and an inspiration. And the manner in which Muir did his camping was added encouragement to Mills. Muir had spent most of his life in the open with the minimum of equipment—a notebook, tin cup, geologic pickaxe, tea, cheese, and hardtack; he scorned a tent, would not be bothered with a blanket, and never carried firearms. A fir thicket and a fire were all he needed for comfort and complete enjoyment of the wildest country. He had walked a "thousand miles to the Gulf," explored the mountains of Utah and Nevada for three years, adventured in Alaska, and made records of unexplored glaciers, one of which in his honor is called Muir Glacier. He was fifty, but in the full flood of his career, with many happy and splendid experiences still to come.

Muir was impressed with Mills's enthusiasm for Nature, but was by no means satisfied with the deductions which the boy had made from his observations. He urged Mills to systematize his already extensive knowledge of wild life, and to learn to write and speak convincingly, make others see and feel it as vividly as he had. He felt the young man had possibilities worth developing, not only for his own greater happiness, but for the help that he could give in the cause which Muir was championing so ardently for the preservation of wild life and scenic beauty. He did not hesitate to put all this before Enos in stirring words:

"You've your life ahead of you, Mills, and you can make it worth a great deal to America. She needs someone who can write and speak with authority, if her wild beauty is to be saved for future generations. From your knowledge of the forest, you have seen that it doesn't take long for the selfish or the ignorant to bring about irreparable destruction. But the world doesn't know this. You must tell them, tell them that we are cutting down and burning up the forests of the West so fast that we'll lay this continent as waste as China, in a few generations. And the people need these beneficial influences; the poetry of Nature makes better citizens of us all. The mountains are fountains, not only of rivers of soil, but of men. But there are so few who have seen this for themselves, lived close to the heart of Nature and heard her story. You have done this, and you must take your stories of the Rockies to people choked up in cities, urge them to see the wild places of the West, arouse their interest in preserving this primeval beauty for their children and their children's children."

Thus it was that Muir gave definite purpose to Mills's talents, directed the trend of his life. Mills frequently expressed the debt he owed the great naturalist, for encouraging him learn to write and to speak about the mountains, as well as to guide people over the trails.

His contact with Muir had done more than fill him with a desire to write, to learn to correlate his information so he could give it to the world. It incited him to "see the wild places of America, the grand side of the continent," as Muir called the Pacific Coast. In the next six months he visited the Redwoods, Muir Woods, Death Valley, the Yosemite Valley, and the Sequoias. He saw the Big Trees in bloom, in late February, their tops clouded with pale yellow blossoms while the trees stood ankle-deep in snow; and he returned in the moonlight to feel the magic of their fascinating shadows on the snowy forest floor.

This was a few months before the Sequoia Park was created, and he heard many hot discussions concerning the desirability of making a national park in California, so remote from civilization. Although the oldest and largest living things on earth, it was a matter of debate whether the Big Trees were of sufficient value to make them worthy of being set aside for a national park. Mills was deeply impressed after his visit to the region, seeing trees thirty feet in diameter and more than two hundred feet high, interspersed with huge younger trees that seemed only slender pyramids by comparison. As Lincoln had said about Niagara Falls, he felt "their power to incite reflection and emotion" was their greatest charm. After having seen a number of trees wrecked and sawed into lumber and learned their vast age, reaching up into thousands of years, he was struck with the age-old experiences through which they had lived. Almost immune from insect pests and with a thick, semi-fire-resisting bark, they yet had experienced repeated injuries, shocks from lightning, and even fire scars, one showing a scar of nearly a thousand years before which had taken three hundred years to heal.

While in Yosemite Valley, he followed Muir's suggestions and studied glaciation. He had an excursion into Hetch-Hetchy and camped in Tuolumne Meadows. For two days in succession as he climbed up to have the view from the summit of

Mount Hoffman, then crossed Mono Pass and had a visit to Mono Lake and the nearby craters.

Unending were the impressions gathered, notes made, campfires built in primeval forests, and glorious nights in the open. Unhurried, he went from one interest to another, seeking out the striking features of topography and scenery. He was gathering related facts now, correlating his observations, as well as adventuring to the fullest. He crossed desert scenes to Virginia City and Reno, and finally took the train back to San Francisco to await a day when Muir could go with him up Mount Tamalpais.

There was more talk between the two of the serious need of national parks, especially in California, where the encroachment of commercial interests were endangering forests, streams, and scenery. Muir put the task upon Mills of helping in this great work for the nation. To a boy of twenty this must have looked tremendous, but the seed took root, for Mills's nature was fertile soil for the development of an idea, once it possessed him.

Enos went on with his adventuring, seeing Death Valley after heavy rains had spread a sudden burst of bloom—that magic of the desert; he followed the coastline down to San Diego and visited the nearby islands. He remembered Muir's advice about seeing new country, "Go with someone who knows if you can; if not, go alone."

It was a thoroughly aroused boy who returned to Long's Peak, fired anew with his enthusiasm for getting more people into the wilderness, and stimulated by Muir's suggestions for continued development of his nature interests. He was thrilled as always by the return to his cabin; he would soon be old enough to file on that hundred and sixty acres and secure a patent on the tract that had become so dear to him. Of course he wondered if there would be any bluebirds nesting near him. Would "Little Blue" return? He tells us in "Bird Memories of the Rockies":

"I paused just long enough to see that there was a nest of baby bluebirds in the old place, then hurried in to examine some papers. Leaving the cabin door open, I took a seat at the table. Suddenly there was a flutter of wings, and a bird alighted on my shoulder, then on the table. He was looking up into my face with worshipful satisfaction.

"'Are you Little Blue?' I asked. 'Are those your babies in the nest?'

"The answer was the low, sweet, whispered warble—the bluebird's song of love and memory."

Yes, he was glad to be home, with his friends and the scenes that he loved best. He had gained much confidence within the year, felt equal to any emergency on Long's Peak. He could devote his thought and energies to the needs of his party, endeavoring to keep them alert, cheerful, and interested in his bits of information. Climbing was second nature to him, but he did not forget the fundamentals which each new climber would have to learn; deliberateness was the first essential, suitable diet before and while climbing made the climb easier, while appropriate clothing was always to be considered. He early cautioned that "straw hats, shawls, umbrellas, or any article of clothing easily plucked by wind or tree limbs should be left behind—it might be anyway."

He mentioned among the qualities that produced skill in climbing, "good nature, lung capacity, endurance, and alertness"; yet one did not have to be an athlete to make the summit, for "successful climbing is done mostly with the head." For safety, success, and the maximum of satisfaction, he recommended that not more than five persons attempt the ascent together.

In order to keep the party together, and prevent those at the rear yelling "Wait," while those in the lead called "Come on," he occasionally stopped and called attention to a squirrel harvesting its cones, adding that squirrels are the greatest tree-planters in the world. Only a small proportion of the seeds being eaten, a large number sprouted and grew into forests. Or he would point out glacial boulders, "marbles of the Ice Age," and picture the scene as it looked some millions of years before. Such comments not only brought the party together, but gave all a source of interest along the trail, once their imagination was stirred to look around them. It eliminated much extraneous conversation.

For as Muir says: "Nature's sources never fail. Like a generous host, she offers her brimming cups in endless variety, served in a grand hall, the sky its ceiling, the mountains its walls, decorated with glorious paintings and enlivened with bands of music ever playing."

It is necessary for a guide to make the introduction to Nature, to be the key that unlocks her storehouse, the interpreter who translates a foreign language. Not all of Mills's guiding was confined to Long's Peak, though that trip offered the most for one day's varied and compelling experiences.

A gentleman came along who was interested in beaver. Enos offered to show him beaver work. They visited three colonies, seeing a variety of dams, houses, canals, tree cuttings, and picturesque ponds. The visitor was intensely impressed, and during the excursion asked forty-seven questions about beaver life and work, all but three of which Enos answered. Two months later the gentleman sent some friends of his to see beaver work, and with Enos they spent the entire day in the Moraine beaver colony.

But the short seasons of guiding were not lucrative, and suddenly, in September, 1890, we find Enos enrolling in Heald's Business College, San Francisco, embarking on what was to him, no doubt, laborious work in bookkeeping and typewriting. Mr. W. A. Clark, one of the owners of the Anaconda, had offered him a position as secretary at a hundred and twenty dollars a month. It was an opportunity for new experience and a promising future. The business college, however, was probably a dull existence for the boy, lacking the stimulating discussions of his associates at Butte.

The environment around San Francisco offered much to relieve the tedium of the stuffy, confining classroom, and he made many opportunities to see more of the seashore and mountains. Muir was constantly inspiring him to see more of the wonderlands of the West, directing his reading and his thought toward unexplored country. He urged Enos to express his ideas on paper, and, even more, to learn to speak in public, emphasizing the fact that he could not begin too young to acquire the confidence necessary to address an audience. Muir never acquired that confidence, a handicap which he often felt in his campaigning for public measures.

The influence of Muir's words must have had immediate results, for in January, 1891, Mills made a talk on forestry in San Francisco, or, as he termed it, "attempted to make one."

But it was a beginning, and the failure, if it was such, did not stop him.

Early spring found Enos back in Butte, where the position with Mr. Clark was awaiting him. It promised permanent, well-paid work, and as a business proposition was a good thing, but after a few weeks the call of the out-of-doors became irresistible.

When he announced his intention of going on a camping trip, his friends thought he must be crazy. To give up a good job and go off into the wilds! Mr. Clark tried to dissuade him, saying, "You're the right kind of young man for Butte, Mills. Stick to mining and you can go as far as you like."

Enos thought differently. He was twenty-one now, and knew what he wanted to do. With a roll of blankets, a map, and a few provisions he started to walk to Yellowstone. He took his time, spent ten days on the trip, and missed little along the way. He remained for seven months, studying the glaciation, geology, geysers, and innumerable natural formations of the Park. The wildlife population in all its variety offered the finest opportunity for study anywhere in the world. The region had been a wildlife preserve for nearly twenty years. Animals had increased and become fearless under this protection, and as yet the bears had not become demoralized by the garbage dumps, miscellaneous feeding and teasing of tourists. It was indeed a wonderland of beauty, mystery, and adventure. Mills came in time to see it at its best, and at an age to appreciate it to the fullest. His reading had given him a background of knowledge of its wonders, from Colter's early discovery and unbelieved stories of the geysers on down through the years of continued exploration.

He had lively scrambles around Amethyst Mountain, studying the petrified forests, thrilled by the geologic stories in the twelve fossilized forests, one above the other, buried at different periods by volcanic eruptions. These remained to him the greatest single attraction in the Park, unmatched in its powers to stir the imagination and rebuild the past. He had a jolly time locating Two Ocean Pass, dividing its waters between the Atlantic and Pacific slopes, because the confusion of topography and water sheds was not indicated on his map.

He made a reverent pilgrimage to the historic spot, at the

junction of the Gibbon and Firehole Rivers, where the celebrated camp of 1870 decided the fate of Yellowstone. Here Cornelius Hedges had proposed that the region be set aside by the Government, and the magnificent national part idea was born—by a campfire in the wilderness. The Park became a reality in less than two years—the first scenic national park in the world.

He had the good fortune to meet General Hiram M. Chittenden, whose life was so intimately connected with the development of the Park and its road and trail system. Chittenden was directing the cutting of trees at a point now famous as Lake View, from which, perhaps, the finest view of glorious Yellowstone Lake is to be had. He was the first to propose that the excess of elk and other game be distributed in other wildlife preserves over the country. Chittenden's "The Yellowstone National Park" is probably the most complete source book for a history and description of the region.

Enos was constantly seeing sights that reminded him of his own Estes Park country. The tree-sprinkled, grassy area lying to the east of Mount Washburn, along the Lamar River, impressed him as the most charming and park-like of all. The roughest and most scenic section visited was around Sylvan Pass; while Yellowstone Canyon, with its richly blended coloring and beautiful Lower Falls, left lasting memories. Everywhere the brilliant and varied flowers gave a finishing touch to the superb scenes.

In July, Enos had an opportunity to join a United States Geological Survey party, and decided to stay on in Yellowstone instead of returning to Long's Peak for the summer. The surveying was full of interest, exploring every section of the Park, and discussing these experiences with an intelligent group of men. There were lively times, too, making close acquaintances with bears, Enos always assuring his companions that there was nothing to be afraid of as long as one did not disturb their normal activities. He frequently led the camp out for a close-up, charging the bear himself to stir up a little action. After the first counter-charge and "woof, woof," Mills holding his ground at a safe distance, the bear would return to its previous occupation. But in their hasty retreat the camp was seldom convinced that the bear wasn't still pursuing.

Many of his observations of these well-behaved bears, both black bear and grizzly, have been recorded; their play, dignity, resourcefulness, intelligence, courage—and self-defense if need be—filled him with the keenest admiration, and their habits and customs afforded interesting and absorbing study.

On one occasion, at least, he learned something of their aggressive nature in the face of undue temptation. Mills had been sent on horseback through the woods to Norris for emergency provisions. On the way back to camp, he stopped to watch a number of black bears. He says: "they sniffed and sniffed and one hurried up to make closer acquaintance with the pony. This formerly tame beast changed to wildness and tried tree climbing. At the same time one of the bears started climbing the pony to investigate a slab of bacon behind the saddle. But the pony went into high and headed for camp without a thought for forest conservation."

Along with the experiences which Enos enjoyed in the Yellowstone was the vision of the larger usefulness of the Park for educational purposes, a program which his later writings helped to develop. Exploring wilderness scenes and meeting their exacting demands was the best, a real education.

Before returning to Long's Peak in the summer of 1892, Mills made a brief visit to Alaska.

Alaska welcomed Mills in a manner befitting his adventurous soul. Tramping the shore of Glacier Bay looking for glaciers, he found them—living, moving mountains of ice and snow, sending off newborn bergs into the sea. One of these large, though young, icebergs broke ponderously on the bay, bowed profoundly, bobbed up, and rolled over with a lurch. The high wave that it sent far up the shore threw driftwood about like a flood. Mills was carried along with it and pitched headlong at the line of high tide.

Not discouraged by the wetting received, he followed the shoreline around the deeply indented bay, noting some of the strange cargoes that some of these floating ice palaces carried; boulders large and small were embedded in the ice; sand, gravel, fallen trees, and even bird's nests, were being transported.

Coming upon a big berg becalmed in a small harbor, its

snout inclined against the shore, he concluded to climb it. It rose fifty or sixty feet above the water, with a nearly level, plateau surface. What most interested him was the pile of logs embedded in one side of the berg, broken spruce that probably had been swept down upon the glacier by a snowslide. He decided to spend the night on this berg, planning to leave it quickly if it started out to sea. He might have to swim, but the shore was close. The logs burned well and with his bearskin and a blanket he lay down to sleep, and did! Sunrise found him still on the berg, but its apparent restlessness with the change of wind warned him not to linger. When he was less than a quarter of a mile along the shore, the berg pulled out to sea.

On one glacier vegetation was growing in the soil of a miniature rock garden—alpine gentians, yellow avena and purple primroses in bloom. A flock of rosy finches was feeding nearby.

Two years later, Mills returned to Alaska, to look again upon that dazzling spectacle of glaciers, as well as to explore farther inland. The whaling vessel that brought him up that mountainous coastline from Sitka had nosed along for days through fog. Finally, when the captain judged they were opposite the inlet to Muir's Glacier, he hove to and dropped a boat containing Mills and two Indians. The Indians paddled for shore and the whaler went on its way.

Suddenly the fog curtain lifted, revealing floating icebergs to right and left putting out to sea. Occasionally a heavy, towering mass of ice collapsed, creating terrific explosions in the water and sending rings of violent waves rushing toward every part of the bay.

Amid all this the little boat moved forward, the Indians munching dried fish eggs as they worked at the paddles. They looked on with interest, but without Mills's enthralled enthusiasm, fortunately, since the onrush of the great waves, coming from all possible directions, made the traffic dangerous. They kept the boat about a quarter of a mile from the ice cliffs where bergs were launched and berg waves started. Heading for a distant inland channel, they were at length in a stretch of open water, where the waves did not reach them, with only one huge berg near, and that floating quietly.

Deceiving calm! Suddenly the boat was flung high into the air. Mills looked down for a terrific moment on top of the mass of ice; the next instant, on a mighty wave, they were rushing shoreward and flung sixty feet above high-water line. An alder thicket modified the shock, but the bow of the boat was stove in against one boulder, while its back was broken over another.

The three men dragged themselves out of the thicket, drenched to the skin—the Indians still munching fish eggs—and stood staring at the retreating wave which carried away all their stores and bedding.

While the Indians built a fire of driftwood, Mills studied the scene. The berg that had wrecked them had risen from the bottom of the bay at least a thousand feet in advance of the visible portion of the ice-front. This submarine berg was a deep blue, but changed rapidly to white. The bay seemed to hold all the ice in the world. Back of the ice cliffs fronting the bay the towering mountains rose dazzling white.

Mills had planned to study Muir Glacier while waiting for the excess of snow to clear from the Chilcoot Pass Trail. But he had landed in Yakutat Bay. The wave which had wrecked him had also flung up hundreds of fish among the willows and alders. These the Indians were cooking, giving little concern to the loss of all their provisions. The boat could be repaired with considerable time and effort. All the rest of the day the three went salvaging along that wild shoreline and by night had assembled repair material—broken boxes and their precious nails, rope, tin cans, and the green and invaluable skin of a wolf that evidently had been killed by a high wave throwing him against the boulders.

For three days, while the Indians worked repairing the boat, Mills explored the glaciers. Everything was on a stupendous scale. Climbing to a commanding point, the distance seemed an immense snow desert with here and there a peak piercing its heavy strata of white. Snowy mountains, glaciers, and icy peninsulas edged the bay. Avalanches crashed down upon the glaciers, echoing and re-echoing in the ice-bound canyons. But the region was not without life. A grizzly crossed the scene one day, lingering to watch a snow slide take its meteoric course. A group of bighorn sheep was seen, and ptarmigan were numerous.

The Indians, meanwhile, had repaired the boat after a fashion and set out to get supplies in an Indian camp down the coast. Mills, a lone castaway now, might have awaited their return with some anxiety. But instead he continued to watch the exhibits of glaciers and icebergs, and to visualize the reconstruction of the landscape through glacial action.

The rescuers returned about midnight, and three hours later in two boats the party was dodging icebergs far down the bay. Once out on the main coast again, a passing steamer was signaled and Mills and the two Indians were taken aboard. A few days later found them at the foot of the Chilcoot Pass Trail, as Mills has told in "Launching Icebergs," in "Romance of Geology."

The most thrilling adventure of these Alaska days, however, has never been made a matter of record. Before reaching Chilcoot Pass, his Indian guides deserted and Mills walked the more than two hundred miles to Juneau, through unknown wilderness and living off the country. The Indians had managed in some way to get possession of the supplies, and it is probable that their repeated threats of desertion had demanded every dollar Enos possessed. At any rate, Mills got back to civilization and worked for a dollar and a half a day until he could save enough to pay his passage back home.

A Crowded Pattern

"For him the old world molds aside she threw,
    And choosing sweet clay from the breast
    Of the inexhausted West,
With stuff untainted shape a hero new."
    Lowell

The late winter of 1893 found Mills at home at Long's Peak, with ambitions to travel to Chicago and see the World's Fair. The little mining town of Ward, some twenty-five miles southward, offered possibilities for making a stake, and in that direction he set off with a roll of blankets.

The ground was deeply covered with snow, and, shortly after starting, a blinding snowstorm came on, adding greatly to the difficulties of travel. Mills was without snowshoes, and the walking was slow and exhausting. Stopping to rest against a fallen tree, he dozed off for a moment. A snap of a twig wakened him suddenly, as a lion disappeared into the woods a short distance away.

Backtracking the lion, he found the beast had been trailing him at a safe distance the greater part of the day, had circled him whenever he had stopped to rest, and while he slept had climbed the fallen tree and looked down upon him. Mills was traveling without a gun, but such was his knowledge of wild animal nature, he had no fear of being attacked. He knew the lion to be especially curious concerning man's actions, often slyly following the hunter or prospector, without any aggressive intentions. Although something of a coward, he nevertheless is a patient and persistent trailer, as Enos found in backtracking him that day.

Darkness came on as Enos continued his journey, and after wandering for hours through rough, mountainous, snow-covered country, the light from a little log cabin among the pines was a cheering sight. The kindly welcome extended by James H. Bunce was characteristic of mountain hospitality, and though they had never met before, the audacity of anyone traveling in that kind of weather was sufficient introduction for the old mountaineer.

Enos had had a long and tiring day, but he found himself entertained until two o'clock in the morning by this former mayor of Louisville, Kentucky. Among his varied and stirring experiences, Bunce had run a line of packet steamers on the Ohio and Mississippi Rivers, but at the end of the Civil War, with broken health and finances, he had moved to Colorado. His hobby was keeping out of debt. He had recommended to the school district of Lyons, which was heavily in debt and already overtaxed, that the school year be shortened until the indebtedness was paid, saying, "It will not do to let children learn the erroneous lesson that it is necessary to go in debt in order to secure the good things of life." His philosophy was helpful, his judgement on questions of the day sane and practical, and his influence in the region of permanent good. The little "Bunce Schoolhouse" still bears his name.

Throughout his mountain rambles, Enos was often meeting these rich and sturdy characters, living their isolated, independent lives, "their best days" as they sometimes called them, away from the cities' mad rush and struggle for existence. The mountaintop mines of Colorado, though often lonely spots through the long winter, were scenes of contentment. They attracted men of travel and experience, and well educated, who were in touch through books and papers with the current thought of the day.

Life in these high elevations, 8,500 to 10,500 feet above sea level, sometimes presented new and novel features. During summer thunderstorms the air might be so overcharged with electricity that the cook had to remember "hands off," whether the dinner scorched or not. Supplies were taken up in summer in sufficient quantities to last all winter, about seven months. These consisted mostly of canned goods of the best brands and suitable variety. To boil potatoes or beans took about twice the time it did at sea level.

The working shifts in the mines were from eight to ten hours, and the work was done under difficulties, for everything inside and out was frozen. In drilling water holes, salt had to be put in the water to keep it fluid. The air was so bracing that the men were always on their toes and thoroughly fit.

After six months at Ward, Enos went on to Chicago. The White City by the Lake was as exquisite as a vision and almost

Enos at the Chicago World's Fair, 1893.

as evanescent. For the first time in America there existed a planned and perfected architectural beauty on a grand scale without a jarring note—a World's Fair worthy of the name. Buildings of harmonious charm stood in a frame of gardens, with artificial lakes, canals, fountains, statues, and studied vistas designed to complete the scheme of loveliness. Looking upon the graceful arches, white towers, friezes, domes, columns against the color of the Lake, the impressive beauty aroused in Mills "inexpressibly glorious feelings, as though listening to inspiring music."

Through and about the exposition surged a multitude, drawn, like its exhibits, from the whole world. A rare opportunity to see human nature in all its moods. The priceless collections, displaying the best of man's inventive genius and his mechanical and industrial achievements in our own country, as well as the startling exhibits from faraway lands, were a liberal education.

It was something to look back upon and talk about for years to come; it was a standard by which all future expositions would be judged. Enos planned his itinerary homeward to include a stop in Kansas to visit his family. Ella and Sarah had married, Belle was teaching, Naomi had died. The brothers had grown up to lusty lads. Changes in his parents were unapparent, but what changes they must have seen in him! From the sickly boy of fourteen, he had developed into a hardy mountaineer. To his mother he enthusiastically unrolled the scroll of the past nine years.

The years following 1893 were crowded with activities of many types—with guiding, writing, speaking, and business. But with it all, there were months each year spent in tramping and camping, not only in his own State, but all over the country. There were trips by horseback and afoot, by stage, train, boat, and bicycle; desert, plain, mountain, and seashore became familiar landmarks. Among his river trips were adventures on the Missouri-Mississippi from source to sea, on the Ohio, the Connecticut, the Columbia, and the Colorado. Two long remembered trips were days spent camping with John Muir. But most of his exploring was done alone, frequently repeating his journeys to verify the observations made.

During the early nineties Mills came in touch with Robert W. Johnson, then of Denver, and the companionship that resulted enriched the lives of both. The two had many camping trips together in the mountains around Estes Park. Johnson has written a delightful summary of these days in the Preface to Mills's "The Rocky Mountain National Park."

Most of Mills's time, during these summers, was devoted to strenuous guiding. He did more than take people to the top of Long's Peak. He expanded into all the bypaths of natural history, drawing on the live material which the trail so abundantly afforded. Unconsciously, at first, he developed a new phase of the work—nature guiding. It was not enough just to answer questions on the geology, the tree and plant life, the name of a flower; he ever endeavored to arouse the interest of those who did not even see these, to him, story-filled wonders. The life history of the lodgepole pine, the habits of the water ouzel, the biography of a boulder, or the manners and home life of the bighorn sheep, were subjects of endless interest and the appeal of the out-of-doors.

He urged people to go out and see these things for themselves, outlined trips that would show them the best that the region afforded, directed them to the most striking examples of beaver work, or told them where a hummingbird would be found at home.

The importance of outdoor life and recreation became an obsession with him. He felt that the prejudices of the human mind were largely due to incorrect knowledge of nature history, to undeveloped condition, as well as prolong life. "Good health is like a hat in a windstorm; you must fun for it across the country or it will get away," he often quoted, or, in his own version:

> "No matter the extent of your learning,
> No matter your gold or your birth,
>   If you want to be strong,
>   And enjoy this world long,
> You must stand with your feet on the earth."

In the fall of 1895, Mills made his first real forestry address in Kansas City. In February, 1896, he was called upon the substitute for a speaker at a teachers' convention in Linn County, Kansas, near his birthplace. He chose for his subject his well-prepared theme "Peru," and according to the newspaper comments had "the rapt attention of everyone present." And he received twenty-five dollars.

In the summer of 1896, Mills began reporting Estes Park society news to the "Denver Times and Republican," and so well was this received that it became a definite assignment, lasting through seven or eight years. There were descriptive articles of the scenic attractions, beginning in 1897, illustrated with views of the region. It was about this time that he gave a talk on "Evolution" before an Estes Park audience, and on the Fourth of July delivered an oration on "The Growth and Prospects of Liberty" at a general gathering of some hundred and fifty people.

There were various miscellaneous contributions to other papers about 1899. "A Plea for Good Roads" in a Linn County, Kansas, paper, as well as "Beyond the Rockies—a Glance at Scenery from Denver to Butte," "The Burning Anaconda Mine," and, in the "Loveland Reporter Herald," "An Opinion on Ingersoll." In 1901, an article on "Vaccination" appeared in the "Anaconda Standard," and another on the "Louisiana Purchase" in the "Butte Miner."

The winter of 1896-97 was spent working in the mines at Victor and Cripple Creek, Colorado, lately come into prominence, chiefly through the discoveries of Winfield Scott Stratton. At the Independence Mine, Mr. Stratton directed Enos where to put in a round of holes. Stratton had a hunch that they were close to a body of rich ore. He was right, for after the blast they returned and found they had uncovered a veritable bonanza which eventually yielded over a million dollars' worth of gold.

Cripple Creek, that only a few years before had been the home of the cowboy and the coyote, soon came to look like a wood and stone crazy-quilt in its oddly assorted architecture. Substantial office buildings and palatial dwellings were hastily erected on the corrugated mountainside, alongside crude huts and "pasteboard" houses that often sat obliquely to the zigzag streets.

There were representatives of every climb and every profession, looking for a "Short, Northwest Passage" to fortune, and prospecting took precedence over any and all other occupations. As the fashion of plunging waned, someone looked under the floor of the Hotel Victor and discovered a gold lead. It was found to extend under the heart of the city, and shaft houses soon displaces dwellings. By leaning over the hotel balustrade, one could watch drilling in the Gold Coin Mine, that soon became one of the best producers in the camp.

Wherever he was, Mills found congenial associates. In Cripple Creek it was the old prospector Lou Crandall, whose daring and skillful escape from Indian pursuers Mills tells in "Waiting in the Wilderness," in the chapter "A Blind Guide." Mills was always stirred by the experiences of these pioneer characters, admiring their mastery of woodcraft more than their skill or luck in mining or prospecting. His genuine appreciation of that quality of the frontiersmen which gave them the ability to become masters of their environment was probably of value to him in his character analysis of wild animals—also pioneers.

When in Denver, Mills often dropped into the editorial rooms of his newspaper friends, Arthur Chapman and Earl

Harding, or J. P. McGuire, of "Outdoor Life." In Estes Park he early came in touch with other writers during their summer residence; William Allen White, Dr. John Timothy Stone, Eugene Fitch Ware, William Herbert Carruth, and Walt Mason, as well as many others who had cottages in various sections of the Park and returned year after year.

It was a busy, strenuous life; summers spent in guiding, greatly increasing the numbers of Peak trips each year, encouraging women and children to climb and making it safe and easy for them to do so; mining in Colorado and Montana during the winter months; with tramping and exploring new country whenever his time and means would allow. Writing and speaking, which were to be his major pursuits, were developing more slowly. At one time he considered studying law, but gave up the idea.

In late May, 1900, Mills left Butte bound for the Paris Exposition. He mentions making a talk in Chicago in June, probably on forestry. With a ticket to New York via Washington, D.C., he saw something of the Capital, and brief glimpses of Baltimore and Philadelphia. A few days were spent in New York City seeing the big attractions, especially the Museum of Natural History. Another talk was made here, in New York.

Sailing June 6 on the St. Paul, seven days were spent in the passage to Southampton. Now he was to see the scenes he had read of so often and dreamed of so fondly; now "the birthplace of Shakespeare, the home of Burns, the glories of France, and the historic ruins of Rome were at last almost in sight." In the month that followed he covered an amazing amount of territory, and in a letter to his sister strikes the keynote of historic interest wherever he went. With the limited time and money at his disposal, he made a remarkable tour of five countries and saw something of the impressive exhibits of the Paris Exposition. Three days were spent in London, seeing her beautiful parks, her historic palaces, and her treasures of sculpture and art; then across the Channel, and four hours by rail "through green and flowers, scenes touched by Joan of Arc," to Paris. He was impressed by Millet's "Gleaners" and the Venus de Milo in the Louvre. On July 4 he saw the statue of Lafayette unveiled. He visited Versailles and then jumped over "three hundred miles of red poppies" to scenic Switzerland. The Blue Rhine,

Lake Lucerne, and the St. Gothard Tunnel engage his interest, then on to Venice, Florence, and Rome. He climbed Vesuvius to the rim of the crater, while fire, ashes, lava and smoke were belched forth; the ancient splendor of Pompeii was reviewed. After a short stay in Geneva, he returned to England, visited Stratford, took a hurried trip through Scotland, lingering around the birthplace of Burns, fascinated by the surrounding scenes and their association with the life and lines of the poet whom he had long admired. The English Lake country was a beautiful ending for his happy holiday. On July 14 he sailed from Southampton, on the St. Louis.

While Mills was in Paris he read in the Paris edition of the "New York Herald" that a fire was raging on the eastern slope of Long's Peak. He cabled Washington, urging action. But the fire was allowed to burn itself out, destroying more than a thousand acres of fine forest. Another fire in the region that summer did enormous damage on the South Fork of the Thompson River and along the Flattop Trail, amid some of the most magnificent stands of forests. The first fire had been started by burning logs left neglected, the second by a campfire. Both were utterly inexcusable.

When Mills returned to Estes Park in August, his thoughts were more on the protection of American forests than the sights to be seen in foreign lands. After visiting the scenes of desolation around his home, the determination to start propaganda to prevent such needless waste started him on a program of forestry conservation of his own. Whenever opportunity afforded, he gave talks on the subject, dwelling on the beauty of the primeval forests and their inspirational influences as well as their economic value. He felt that if a more widespread appreciation of trees could be engendered, careless fires would never start, and ruthless cutting of timber in the rare and poetic wilderness scenes would be controlled. "Our Greatest Friend and Most Valuable Resource—The Forest," became his constant theme.

The Park was taking on some new development with the years: a telephone line connected it with the outside world, and a number of stores were adding to the expansion of business. It was none too soon to save the region. Local people must be aroused if the proper sentiment was to be fostered among the tourist visitors who formed the larger part of the population in summer.

Beaver had been in danger of extermination for some time. Mills had been actively championing the beaver for its value, both as an object of interest and as a conserver of the water supply. Wild life, too, had diminished through years of hunting, and what remained was less frequently seen because of the inroads of an unfriendly civilization. Mills was constantly preaching that all wild life would become friendly if not molested, and that a study of its habits and customs was a happy source of mental relaxation. But, like many another reformer, he was years ahead of his time; in fact, he was in the vanguard of the conservation movements of the coming century.

During the summer of 1901, Mills negotiated with Carlyle Lamb for the purchase of the Long's Peak House property—the hundred and sixty acres adjoining his homestead tract which he had acquired in a patent from the Government a few years earlier. It is probable that his interest in forest and wild life protection prompted his action, although it is also said he took the property partly on an old debt. At any rate, at the age of thirty-one, he embarked on the first business enterprise of his life, and one which was to call for enormous expenditures of money to make it worthy of his hotel ambitions and adequate to serve the peculiar needs of the region. He went in the early fall to Butte, where he was always sure of a job at high wages, to meet immediate demands of the newly acquired property.

At this time the "ranch" consisted of a few scattered log buildings, accommodating between ten and twenty guests. Mills returned in late winter to make some improvements and additions, and to prepare for his first summer of catering to the hotel demands, as well as outdoor requirements, for mountaineering people from all over the world.

He had definite ideas on the subject, good food and good beds being the first essentials, for which there was no substitute, not even scenery. But, in addition, he determined to initiate some new features, never before heard of in the hotel industry. He had brought back from Europe a strong aversion to the tipping system, and characteristically decided that in his hotel, at least, he would try to eliminate the evil. It was run as a "non-tip" house during his lifetime and for some years after.

Other innovations were introduced, governed by environmental factors or in line with his conservation teachings. He established the custom of using a single flower as table decorations in the dining room. He asked his guests and visitors not to pick handfuls of flowers from his premises. This was, then, as new and unheard of as the "non-tipping system." Many so-called nature lovers protested that the flowers were wild and belonged to them as much as to anyone. By tactful explanation that the wild flowers would not multiply unless allowed to go to seed, that careless picking often destroyed the roots, and by repeating this year after year, to constantly changing people, he maintained the natural profusion of bloom in what has ever been one of the finest wild flower gardens in the region.

Although having a general antipathy to signs, Mills also posted his grounds with a notice reading:

Spare The Flowers

Thoughtless people are destroying the plants by greedily picking and recklessly uprooting them.

Keep Colorado a Wild Garden

(Signed) THE OUT-DOOR LEAGUE

A cloth sign Enos kept posted near Long's Peak Inn.

It was, very likely, the first public plea for wild flowers, and if so, the first of a legion. It bore abundant fruit, but slowly. It took a generation for the public to accept the creed that others should be allowed to enjoy the flowers, that a selfish destruction of wilderness beauty would only result in ultimate desolation.

That Mills was expending more time and energy on his conservation work than in getting returns on his hotel investment is evident from the meager returns of one early season, less than two hundred dollars. He had utmost confidence in the region, however, and continued to expand, adding a good log cabin or two, and gradually doing away with tents entirely. Beginning with 1904 the name "Long's Peak Inn" was adopted, and advertising cards printed announcing "trails to dark forests, white waterfalls, snow-edged lakes, old moraines, alpine moorlands, rugged gorges and peaceful dells...the place to get acquainted with the Rockies." Rates for room and board were given at $2.50 to $4 per day; $12 to $20 per week, with the added note, "Conversations with the Proprietor Extra." Whether the latter was suggested by some of his guests, vying with one another to engage his attention, or a humorous means of escape from loquacious callers, it at any rate gave his neighbors and competitors something to talk about, which perhaps is the main purpose of advertising.

In 1903, John Muir wrote, "I hope some day to see your Rockies," a hope that never materialized. But numerous other naturalists did come, doubtless enjoyed unlimited conversations with the proprietor, among them David Starr Jordan, Professor Edward Orton, Jr., Julia Ellen Rogers, Frank M. Chapman, and Vernon Kellogg.

Sharing his homestead cabin was "Scotch." In the spring of 1902, returning home on horseback from some distant exploration, Mills was offered a tiny collie puppy. The gift was in return for some kindness shown, and could not be refused. He was an engaging little puppy and immediately settled down at home in Mills's overcoat pocket, licking his master's hand at every opportunity. He proved a devoted companion on many long and sometimes dangerous mountain trips, and the experiences the two enjoyed together, as told in Mills's "The Story of Scotch," reveal the bond of sympathy and under-

Enos with Scotch,
November 26, 1903.

standing that existed between them.

In June, 1903, two other pets arrived to add to the life of the place. Mills had heard of two bear cubs being at large, after the shooting of their mother. No time was lost in making their acquaintance, but it took a lively scramble to get them into a sack and back to his homestead cabin. After their first meal they became friendly, and, like the little bluebirds, came to depend upon him for their daily rations. They would eat anything that was offered, but preferred apples, even to meat or honey.

Johnny and Jenny were up to all sorts of tricks, but seriously objected to having jokes played on them. Mills had recounted their amusing growing-up days, reminding him frequently of children in their reactions to training, and in all respects evidencing the highest degree of intelligence among the wild life of his acquaintance. They were finally placed in the Denver Zoo, however, because of the difficulty of finding anyone to take care of them during his absences from home.

During the summer of 1902, the exact height of Long's

Peak was accurately determined by the students of the Colorado Agricultural College running a transit line from a Union Pacific bench line near the Thompson River to the summit of the Peak, followed by the United States Geological Survey party running another line from a benchmark at Greeley. While originally estimated as a few hundred feet higher, it was a satisfaction to have the elevation fixed at 14,255 feet, ranking fourteenth in the State, one of forty-three peaks above the fourteen-thousand-foot mark.

Mills continued his guiding on Long's Peak until the end of the summer of 1906. The last season was a full one; thirty-two ascents were made during August, half a dozen being by moonlight. In addition, a daily round trip was made to Estes Park, eight miles distant and fifteen hundred feet down the mountain; commonly on horseback, but occasionally by wagon. The busiest day of all was crowded with two wagon trips and one horseback trip to Estes Park, then a moonlight climb to the summit of the Peak. In a sixty-hour stretch Mills did not sleep or eat. But he was in perfect health, thoroughly familiar with the exacting demands of the work, and enjoyed it. During the past twenty years he had climbed the Peak more than forty times alone, and two hundred and fifty-seven times as guide; he had climbed it every month in the year, and at every hour of the night and day. It would ever remain, to him, the one superb attraction for mountain climbers the world over. After climbing more than two hundred other peaks, he said: "Long's Peak has individuality, it commands magnificent distances, it offers safe and scenic ways up into the cloud and blue, and is exceedingly rich in geology and in plant and animal life. Its climb is free from ice, it has little snowfall, and the wealth of its scenes is won without desperate effort. It is more easily, safely climbed in midwinter than Mont Blanc or the Matterhorn in midsummer. Nature has so distinguished Long's Peak that it is destined to become still more prominent in American outdoor recreation."

Two years after he had last seen Johnny and Jenny, he went to visit them at the Denver Zoo. They were in a large pen with a number of other bears. Regardless of the fact that Johnny was now a big bear also, Mills climbed over the picket fence, calling, "Hello, Johnny." Johnny jumped up wide awake, extending both arms as he stood erect, and gave a few happy grunts of greeting. Mills took hold of his paws and the two danced around in the pen with numerous observers on the outside enjoying the unusual demonstration.

Johnny died in 1925, aged nearly twenty-two, probably as the result of overfeeding from visitors. Jenny is still alive and is reported to be the oldest grizzly in captivity.

Editor's note: For more about Johnny and Jenny, the story is told by Enos in "The Grizzly, Our Greatest Wild Animal" and "Being Good to Bears."

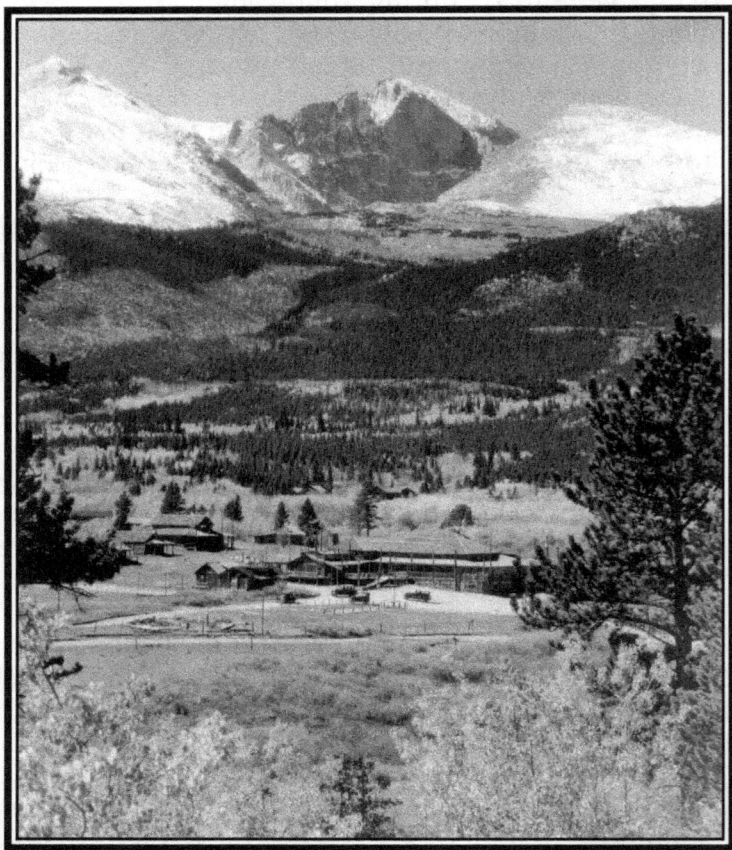

Long's Peak Inn and Long's Peak.

Colorado Snow Observer

"In all sports it falls to the lot of a few men to excel, and in mountaineering this is specially so. The real expert realizes more than his less experienced confreres the smallness of his best efforts, and never is an expedition undertaken without his adding to the almost endless store of technical knowledge that is required if he is safely to indulge in mountaineering. The great mountaineer is the man with all his senses on the alert, and though, despite his comparative insignificance, he may revel in the glories of Nature's most stupendous handiwork, he must never neglect the laws which govern his craft, nor forget for a moment the penalty of neglecting them."

George D. Abraham, "The Complete Mountaineer"

One chapter of Mills's life was closed. With his entering into the hotel business, his mining days were over. He was now to concentrate his energies more entirely on mountaineering, sometimes startlingly daring, which his fifteen years of experience made second nature.

The Estes Park people were accustomed to his winter exploring trips. But in traveling farther from home, when he dropped down into some settlement on snowshoes, he surprised the townspeople who never ventured above timberline in winter.

An unexpected opportunity came to put these lonely explorations to practical and profitable purpose. Mr. L. G. Carpenter, of the State Irrigation Department, was looking for someone to carry out experimental work on the upper slopes of the Rockies, to estimate the snowfall and subsequent water supply for the lowlands. He sent for Mills to come to Denver to talk over the work.

"If I knew the amount of snow on the mountains around Leadville, I could make my report of more value," Carpenter said. "But I haven't been able to get anyone to go over that desolate country in the winter, and I don't know that I should ask anyone to undertake the difficult job of playing snowman for the State."

"It shouldn't be difficult to get the information," Mills answered. "When I'm up that way I will make measurements and send them to you."

"But I need the information at once," Carpenter explained.

"Very well," Mills replied, "I'll see what I can do for you." He went out, purchased a few provisions and started forth in a conventional business suit.

Taking the first train to Leadville, he was soon snow-shoeing over the mountain area that was to supply him with the necessary data. All in the same week he handed Mr. Carpenter his extensive report.

"You've been there and back already, and in those clothes?" Carpenter asked in astonishment, eyeing Mills's city clothes that were somewhat the worse for wear.

"I'll admit I wasn't very suitably dressed," Mills said, "but I knew you were in a hurry, and I wanted to take advantage of favorable weather conditions. For this kind of work it is necessary to make very careful observations. But if the report isn't complete, I will be glad to go back over the ground, for I thoroughly enjoyed the trip and would like to see more of the country."

"It looks to me just what I want," said Carpenter, studying the carefully tabulated notes. "But wasn't there a great deal of snow on the high peaks? According to your report there seems to be an unusual amount in the canyons."

"The high peaks are mostly swept bare of snow. The accumulation is greatest on the middle slopes, especially below timberline, where it is held and protected by the forests."

"That's why we must fight for forest conservation, young man." Carpenter, an expert on this question, smiled at Mills.

"Yes, forests increase and conserve precipitation, prevent erosion and the drying out of the soil, and reduce the chances of snow slides. If forest fires continue unchecked, our streams will soon be dry. You can see in the report that on burnt-over watersheds there is practically no snow accumulated, because the drying winds and exposure to the sun simply eat it up. No one can realize the damage done by fires, aside from the loss of timber, unless he has studied the relation of forests to stream flow. We need to plant more trees and to protect all that we have. Next to water"—he paused to catch Mr. Carpenter's nod—"trees are America's greatest resource; man cannot live without them. In the forest man can sustain himself for days without other resource; he has shelter from storms, wood for his fire, food from the bark and nuts and from the berries and shoots of plants which the forest sustains."

"Yes, all that is true, and we are vitally concerned with the irrigation possibilities afforded by the snowfall on the higher ranges. I am asking you to undertake the investigation. It will require you to cover as much of the territory above timberline as you can safely reach. I want you to make notes on anything likely to be of value to the Department of Agriculture or to the Weather Bureau—and to be careful not to lose your life."

A unique position—"Colorado Snow Observer." There has not been another like it, before or since. For three successive winters Mills traversed the upper slopes of the Rockies and explored the crest of the continent alone. Necessarily he had some thrilling experiences; there were narrow escapes from snow slides and avalanches; perhaps, too, close calls from freezing or starving to death, although of his physical hard-ships he makes little mention. Even when he had to practice arm-swinging and strenuous gymnastics most of the night to keep himself alive, he said that he considered his situation superior to that of people shut up in stuffy houses or ill from the consequences of too much indoor life.

On these excursions he carried a camera, barometer, com-pass, notebook, safety axe, matches and candles with which to start a fire quickly, when dry wood was hard to find. He left all bedding behind, and notwithstanding he was alone and in the wilds, he carried no gun. His food was often only raisins; sometimes chocolate and nuts were added. But his pack had to be kept very light. Owing to the distances covered he often stayed out and up as much as ten days or two weeks at a time, during which he lived happily in sunshine and storm, in blizzard and by campfire, sometimes without seeing another human being. He sums up in the account told in "Wild Life on the Rockies" by saying, "There was an abundance of life and fun in the work."

He had no specially designed clothing for these trips. A fine silk, close-fitting cap, to pull down over his ears, was worn under his felt hat; and silk gloves worn under his heavy mittens gave greater protection in extreme cold, and also allowed him to remove his mittens when taking pictures. His coat was of water-shedding canvas, with numerous deep pockets in which to store his notebooks and instruments. He always carried three separate supplies of matches, two in tin boxes in different pockets and an emergency supply sewed up in waterproof silk.

He covered his special assignments of measuring snowfall or recording the lack of it, studied the topography of the rugged, broken mountaintops and its influence on wind currents and precipitation, made notes on the forest covering of the different watersheds, and observed the general weather conditions. These reports were sent to the Irrigation Department at Denver, and useful information was passed onto the farmers of the State.

The reporter's own interest did not end with the necessary gathering of data; he saw more than wind and water and weather. There was the daily news of the wild animal world which he read in the tracks in the snow; the indifferent movements of the porcupine or the startled leap of a snowshoe rabbit; the family gatherings of ptarmigan, so well camouflaged in white; the solitary trail of a fox that followed the edge of the timberline. And he was often a star witness at a lion's excessive killing. Numerous animals and birds live on or near high peaks the year round, preferring the sunshine of the heights to the shelter of the lower slopes.

Mills commonly dropped down below timberline at night where shelter and wood for a generous campfire could be had. Many nights he dared not sleep because the fire must be frequently replenished. Sometimes, if he was caught in a storm unexpectedly and could not make the shelter of the woods, he dug into a snowbank with his snowshoes and must have felt near kin to the Eskimo.

And always there was the grandeur of towering peaks, which he often went out of his way to climb, the snow draped rocks and trees, dark shadowed canyons, snowy vistas stretching away into space, and ever-changing cloud formations above and, sometimes, below him. He registered these impressions unconsciously, so intensely alert were all his senses. Even in the most dangers of situations, his mental processes took in the whole scene—not only the particular peril involved, but all the contributing factors.

One night he was zigzagging down a narrow canyon in a wild snowstorm when he caught the light from a little cabin tucked away between trees in the lee of an enormous rock. Knocking at the door, he was greeted by a scholarly looking, gray-bearded man and invited into the welcome shelter. Surprised though he was at receiving a caller, true to the Western custom, the host asked no questions.

"Mighty glad to see you, young man, for as a rule I don't see anything human, once the snow comes, until spring takes it away again. You're just in time for supper, too, so make yourself at home."

As Mills removed his wet clothing, he explained who he was and why he was traveling at this hour and season. "But I seldom see a library like this in my wandering over the mountains," he commented as he glanced around the room lined with books.

"It isn't so bad. You see, I never had time to read all I wanted until it came here, three years ago. It took some trying to get them up here, but there isn't one book I could spare. For here there's really time to read, and there's time to think. A man needs to do some of that before he says his final good-bye."

In time the scholar spoke of himself, as the two set before the noble fireplace, piled high with blazing logs. He had been a professor in a Southern college. When the time came to retire, he decided to return to the Rockies, to this spot which he had seen once on a short vacation.

"In the little town where I taught I was always surrounded by people. I thought I'd like to spend a year all by myself, doing just as I liked, arranging my own schedule, getting away from routine. But when the year was up, I stayed on. And now I doubt if I'll ever go back. I'm working on a book of my own. Whether it will ever see print, I can't say, and probably it doesn't matter. I have had lots of fun doing it. I've come to the conclusion that there's a good deal wrong with our system of education, and I'm putting down some ideas and plans that might have value. Anyway, the best of me is in those pages; they represent the conclusions I've reached here in this mountain cabin."

As Mills went on the next day, he hoped he might have more such happy meetings. But the next encounter was of a quite different kind. It was noon of a bitter cold day and he had had a hard, rough trip. As he descended a forested canyon he saw smoke and headed toward it. A man was chopping wood beside a cabin, but snowshoes whisper quietly over the snow, and it was not until he was close that the chopper turned around and saw him. Then he gave a yell that brought his wife to the door and halted Mills abruptly in his tracks.

He had been out for a good many days and nights, and the charcoal with which he blackened his face to protect his eyes from snow glare had become pretty generally distributed. In addition, his contact with the mountains have left various marks on his clothes. His appearance was doubtful, even desperate, but he was not prepared for the wood-chopper's command:

"You clear out o' here!"

"Why, what's wrong with me?" Enos asked gently, not wishing to be taken at the stranger's estimate. From the open cabin door and advertising fragrance of dinner floated out to him. He had not had a meal in a good many hours.

The man was picking up a club, and looked as if he meant to use it, when the old grandmother joined the party, peering curiously at the awful looking tramp who faced them.

"What ails you, Bill?" she exclaimed, chuckling. "Can you see all the young feller wants is a wash and a square meal?"

Her son, still doubtful, approached Mills to give him a closer examination. Grinning, Mills lifted his hat to the two women and above his charcoal-smeared face his bald white-domed forehead and mass of curly red hair showed up. The woodsman grinned, too, while Grandma observed:

"I see your head's above timberline, young man."

"We ain't used to having folks dropped in this time o' year," Bill explained as they were enjoying the good dinner. "And you looked exactly like crazy person, with that face of yours all besmeared, your hat battered and torn, and not a sign of a pack or blankets on you. Where'd you spend the night, anyhow?"

So Mills told them about his job, and his work in measuring the snowfall and making records for the Irrigation Department.

"Sure, we've heard of the 'Snowman,' but I wasn't looking for you to drop down on us like this."

"I'm not as jumpy as Bill, here," Grandma said as Mills prepared to leave. "Once he gets to be my age, he won't be seeing a nigger in every woodpile."

"Well, I'm certainly much obliged to you, ma'am," he assured her. "I was needing that dinner badly."

They were of all sorts, these dwellers in the heights, but

each had individuality and seemed to be getting more out of life than dwellers in cities, Mills thought.

There was a happy evening spent with the more than middle-aged couple whom he found on and out-of-the-way peak—he a retired lawyer who had been Attorney General of Kansas, she a trained physician. They had built themselves a comfortable little home, with a big, attractive living room, bright with flowers, and books to read. They told him they had never seen any better days than they had found right there.

Up at timberline was the cabin of an old woman who was an ardent prospector. Mills was invited to sit by her fire and talk rocks.

"I've staked more than one promising claim," she told him, "and then sold out to men looking for a chance to mine. I'm out with my pick all summer. During winter I read the government reports and studied pamphlets on mining and prospecting. It's a fine life."

Some years later, when she had grown too old for roughing it at timberline, she made postmistress at Hancock. Here Mills met her again and stopped to chat over the days that were past.

"I've a comfortable little home here and folks are awful nice to me, but I'll never be as happy again as I was in my old cabin up among the rocks," she told him.

Perhaps the meeting he enjoyed the most during his years as snow-gauger was the one with Mrs. Harriet L. Wason, known as the poet laureate of the Rockies. Mills had always wanted to know the author of "Letters from Colorado." In the spring of 1903, coming down from the wild San Juan Range, he headed for Creede, a little town of a few hundred citizens, lying some miles northeast of the headwaters of the Rio Grande. He hoped to find a good boarding house here. When not far from the village he met a motherly looking old lady who stopped him for a few words of greeting. In the course of their conversation he told her who he was and what he was doing, and she asked him to walk along home with her. It was a pretty frame cottage standing in a yard full of spring flowers, and inside there were more blooming plants.

"I see you love flowers," Mills said, "and even have some of the wild mountain flowers planted in your yard. And what a fine outlook on the peaks and range!"

"I couldn't live anywhere but here," she answered. "I've

got to have mountains were my eyes can rest on them." She then told him her name and it was that of his long-admired poet.

"You're living just where you ought to live, Mrs. Wason! It's just as you put it in one of your poems:

> 'No narrow street shuts out our sky,
> No human throngs confuse our thought,
> Our boundaries are mountain high
> And these against the blue skies caught;
> While regal piece holds empire sweet
> To where the blue and prairie meet.'"

"Now I know why I liked you the minute I saw you," she smiled back at him. "Talk about casting your bread on the waters!"

The winter of 1903 witnessed two records made in mountaineering at his own home. In February, he climbed Long's Peak, the first winter ascent that had ever been made. And in the same month he crossed them Continental Divide on the Flattop Trail to Grand Lake, which had hitherto been considered impossible in winter. The latter experience he described vividly in "Wildlife on the Rockies."

The same year, in late spring, he had an even more spectacular mountain climbing adventure.

He had climbed a peak near Long's to take some pictures of Long's sheer east precipice, when he was seized with a desire to be on it. Its decent had been made once, with great peril as we know, by the Reverend. E. J. Lamb in 1871. Nevertheless, Mills decided to go on to the summit of Long's by the regular trail and attempt the descent down the eastern, perpendicular wall.

From the top of Long's Peak to Chasm Lake is a drop of some three thousand feet, and, looked at casually, appears sheer precipice most of the way. Snow and ice clung to it that June day; the blue water of the lake showed in patches where the ice had partially melted.

Mills was in perfect physical condition and possessed by his passion for mountain climbing. The fearful descent tempted him. He had with him his ice axe and his camera. Leaving the flat summit, he scrambled cautiously down the steep incline, cutting an occasional foothold in the ice, stopping on a bit of solid rock to examine the step ahead. Unhurried, he took pictures of the views never before photographed. On he went, calm of nerve, yet thrilled as men are thrilled when facing possible death. He was far too expert a mountaineer not to comprehend the peril of what he was doing, but he trusted in his knowledge and in his strength and steady hand.

When he had come down possibly half the distance, he reached a ledge with a little space and stopped to look around. The view of the towering cliff above was sublime. But a sudden roar, followed by a deluge of snow from above, made him crouch quickly against the wall. A small avalanche of stones following the snow was deflected by the outcurving cliff, whirled far into the air over him and into the depths below.

When all was quiet again, Mills scanned the descent immediately below him. It was a precipitous drop. He was shelved. But studying the face of the wall closely, there appeared to be a groove, worn from the trickle of mounting snows. It offered a chance, if he could wedge himself into it. He worked his way down, inch by inch, with perilously slender foot and hand holds. Icy water plunged down from some seventy feet above, spraying a ledge below. With the icy water pouring on his head and trickling down his back, and braced against the sides of the groove, he edged his way down, eventually landing on the ice-covered ledge. It was doubly dangerous here, as he might start an avalanche. Cautiously he slid on, cutting footholds to keep from slipping off, dodging lumps of rotten ice and small stones that kept bombarding him from above. One of the ice-bullets struck him on the head, knocking him into a snowbank, however. He picked himself up uninjured, alive in every fiber of his being. But he seemed to have reached an impasse.

Close by an avalanche was swinging its way down, taking the only cut in the steep rock. It tore past in uneven masses, now heavy, now light. For a few moments Mills studied it. It must be his wild horse, to ride to death or to safety.

Timing the precise instant, he sprang twenty feet and landed on top of the massed and roaring monster, rapidly gathering pace as it went. Crouched on the flying avalanche he sped, deflected this way and that, as rocks turned the flow; moving slowly at moments when the surface flattened, then faster as it inclined; now round a curve, then dropping almost perpendicularly. About him particles of snow and ice hurtled, rocks flew, and the wild chant of the snow-stream thundered in his ears.

Eight hundred feet of this mad ride and the avalanche landed him on the shore of Chasm Lake. He was buried for an instant, but dragged himself out, bleeding from innumerable small cuts, battered and bruised, but happy.

Mills got to his feet, shook as much avalanche out of his clothes and hair as possible, and took the homeward trail. He reached the Inn just as his newspaper friend, Earl Harding, arrived by the stage.

"Where'n thunder you been climbin' this time?" the astonished stage driver inquired. "Look like you'd fallen offen the peak and lit in the lake."

Mills smiled:

"Been out taking pictures and slipped into some water."

He told Harding the story later, and Harding wrote an account which appeared in "Outing" for July, 1904. Otherwise, like many another of Mills's adventures, it might have gone unheralded, save for a few words of comments and a few remarkable pictures. The account has been reprinted in "The Rocky Mountain National Park."

Harding came to the Inn frequently, discussing with Mills the problems of writing. Mills always welcomed critical comment, enjoyed nothing better than reading aloud something on which he was working, getting his hearer's impressions. He never wearied of revising, had the artist's urge for perfection. Harding said of him, "He was so observant that he was his own best critic."

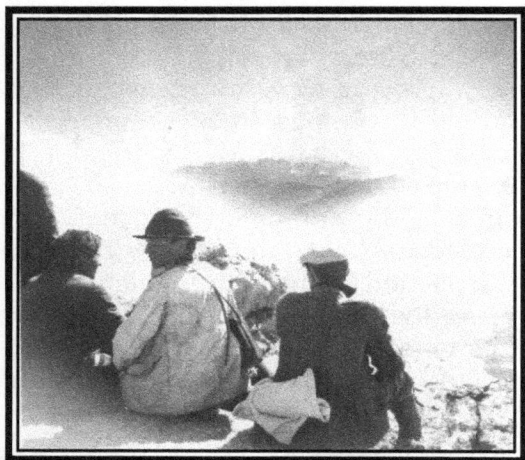

Enos guiding on Long's Peak, looking south from the summit.

Mills was not really interested in performing spectacular feats. He was more concerned with making it worthwhile to other people to climb mountains. Especially he encouraged women and children to climb Long's Peak, wanting them to know the joy of following the trail all the way to the top. He made it safe and easy for them to do so, showing them how to save their energy in climbing, and setting a slow, even pace which would not wear out. He enjoyed taking children up, and their eager, ready questions about the birds and animals delighted him.

Ethel Husted had long been wanting to climb Long's, which she could see from her mountain home fourteen miles away. She had learned to ride horseback at the age of four and had had many camping trips with her father. Before she was ten years old, her father consented to her climbing Long's, and brought her to the Inn for Mr. Mills to guide. Of the trip Mills said:

"She made the climb without assistance, never weakened or faltered, and the climb caused no ill results. Ethel is not only surefooted and strong, but has unusual powers of observation. She examined many things that a child her age would rarely see, and while her comments were those of a child, yet she had the keen and all-seeing eye of a scout. Ethel's life has been a preparation for the feat she so easily accomplished. The trail has given her health, alertness, and courage."

In October, 1903, while in southwestern Colorado, where four states corner, Mills decided to have a look at the Mesa Verde ruins of the cliff dwellers.

He reached the spot in late afternoon. The curiously haunting glamour of these still today unexplained relics of an unknown past and race filled him with wonder. But he was struck to the heart to see vandalism, work of conscienceless curio-seekers, that was all too evident. Suddenly, as he moved among the deserted ruins he caught sight of a shadow falling across a transverse ahead of him. He found it to be that of a blanketed Indian, who stared upon him somewhat grimly.

Mills spoke, greeting him, but he shook his head as though not understanding, and pointed with a frown on his face to the camera slung over the white man's shoulder. Immediately Mills signed that he would not use it, whereupon the Indian smiled and, speaking in perfect English, returned his greeting courteously.

The two shared their campfire and supper that night, talking about the ruins, lamenting that they were being destroyed. Mills remarked that he was going to make an effort to interest the state in having the place protected. It ought to be saved for future generations. He had been surprised to find an Indian on the ground, for he knew these ancient places were feared by the race, as harboring ghosts, spirits of the past. But he no longer wondered when the Navajo told him that he was not only a graduate of Carlisle, but had pursued the study of archaeology in the universities of Europe.

"I live not far from here on the San Juan River," the Indian told him in parting. "Come and see me if you ever return to this vicinity."

Mills hoped that he might sometime be able to accept the invitation. But he had little idea where he would be from month to month. Wherever the Irrigation Department needed more data on a snowfall or the stream flow, there his course lay. He might climb a mountain or go all around one in getting the information he wanted, but so much the better, so far as he was concerned.

It was in a cabin near Canyon City that Mills met two amusing characters. It was an isolated placed on a lively creek, once the haunt of some prospectors, but now the home of two young men with very long hair. They had been there for several months, gathering herbs and allowing their hair to grow. Now that winter was coming on, they intended to go back to civilization, call themselves medicine men, and pass up their concoctions from the herbs and roots as Indian remedies. They would gather crowds at street corners, themselves picturesque in fringed buckskin and beaded moccasins, with a line of talk to fit their appearance and their claims. Mills, tickled, spent the night at the place and gleefully they told him of their plans for the summer's adventures.

But the human and wild life encounters were a slight part of his experiences as a Snow Observer. It was the trail, or rather the regions he traversed where there was no trail, that provided the great adventures, the supreme dangers.

During one winter he walked the crest of the continent— the "snowy range" of Colorado—from the Wyoming line to close upon the New Mexico. He occasionally descended as low as seven thousand feet, and often climbed to the summit of peaks rising 14,000 feet into the sky. On steep, snowy slopes he was alert to the danger of starting snow slides, or being in the path of one that started of its own accord, and always careful to keep his bearings so that he would not become lost if the clouds settled down and obliterated all landmarks or a mirage distorted the landscape. But on one occasion, going into the Uncompahgre Mountains of southwestern Colorado, in late autumn, he was caught in a heavy snowfall without snow shoes and with but little food, and a series of dangerous adventures followed.

In addition to losing his sense of direction, he suffered a night of raw, primitive life. As he tells in "The Spell of the Rockies," in "Alone with a Landslide": "Twenty-four hours of alertness and activity in the wilds, swimming and wading a torrent of ice-water at two o'clock in the morning, tumbling out into the wet, snowy wilds miles from food and shelter, handicapped by a crushed foot and helpless leg, the penetrating, clinging cold, and no fire, is going back to Nature about ten thousand years farther than it is desirable to go. But I was not discouraged—at last the fire blazed."

Remarkable powers of concentration on the thing he was doing doubtless accounted for his ability to meet many seemingly hopeless situations. Also, he had a philosophy of his own, which he states simply:

"Years of training had given me great physical endurance, and this, along with a peculiar mental attitude that Nature had developed in me from being alone in her wild places at all seasons, gave me a rare trust in her and an enthusiastic though unconscious confidence in the ultimate success of whatever I attempted to accomplish out-of-doors."

There are few better adventure stories in literature than these accounts of winter trips on the summit of the Rockies, when all Mills's knowledge and fortitude were brought into play against the elemental forces of Nature. Among these are, "In the Winter Snows" and "Associating with Snow-Slides," in "Rocky Mountain Wonderland"; "Racing an Avalanche," "Mountaintop Weather," "Sierra Blanca," and "In a Mountain Blizzard," in "The Spell of the Rockies"; " Midget, the Return Horse," "Colorado Snow Observer," in "Wild Life on the Rockies, "Snow-Blinded on the Summit," "Winter Mountaineering," "Wind Rapids of the Heights," in "Adventures of a Nature Guide"; "Coasting off the Roof of the World" and "Snow Slides to Start to Finish," in "Waiting in the Wilderness"; "Winter Ways of Animals," in "Watched by Wild Animals"; and " Dweller of Mountaintops," in "Wild Animal Homesteads."

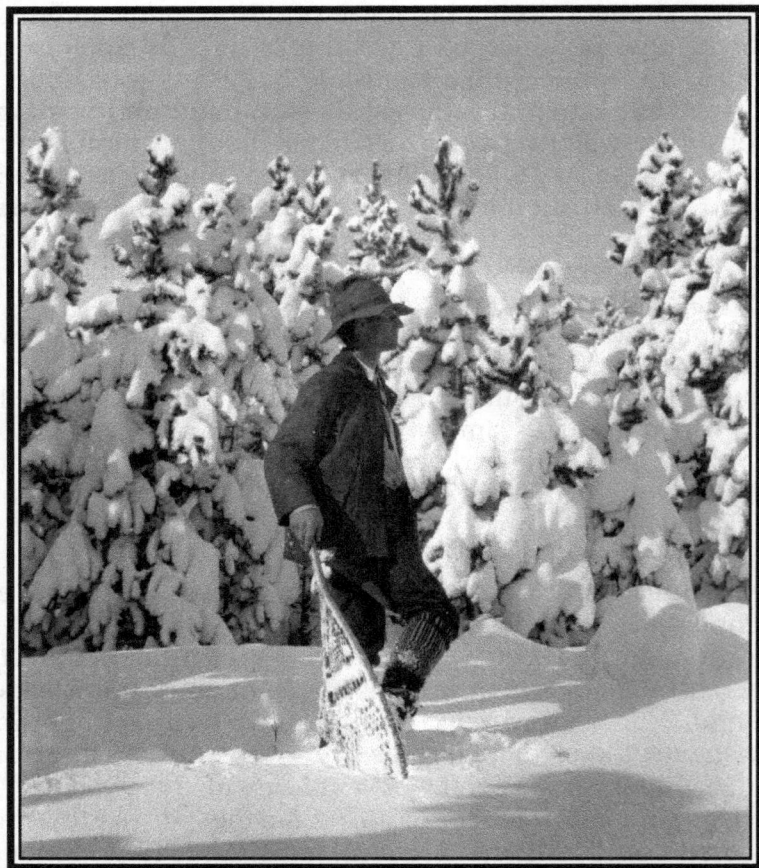

Enos on his snowshoes.

The New Inn

"How happily trees have mingled with our lives! From cave to cottage, the forest has been a mother to our good race. If we should lose the hospitality of the trees and the friendship of the forest, our race too would be lost, and the desert's pale, sad sky would come to hover above a rounded, lifeless world. Friendship is the spirit of the forest."

Enos A. Mills

Mills was lecturing at the Biennial Convention of the General Federation of Women's Clubs in St. Paul, June 4, 1906, when he received a telegram, "Long's Peak Inn burned to the ground."

He hastened home to inspect the ruins of the main building, including the new additions he had made the year before. One or two outlying cabins had escaped, but the loss including almost an entire edition of "The Story of Estes Park," a quantity of table silver and supplies that he had purchased for the coming season, and a large collection of valuable negatives of animals and birds that could not be replaced. There was no insurance.

It was a serious calamity and may have raised some question in his mind as to whether he would continue in the hotel business. The thousands of people who enjoyed his hospitality during the years to follow may well be grateful that he decided to rebuild and start anew.

Borrowing heavily, he at once engaged all the available workmen the community afforded to speed up the work of construction. While the gang brought in the timbers he sat down and drew his plans, which were original in every sense. Instead of using ordinary logs he utilized the fire-killed trees standing on the nearby mountains in such abundance. He selected the most interesting and unusual of these, trees weathered by wind and erosion, twisted and gnarled trees that nevertheless made excellent building materials. The fire that had killed them had also boiled the resinous sap and given them a preservative treatment. Mills had drawn his plans, but carrying them out presented difficulties not anticipated, as he tells in "Sunset Magazine," May, 1921, after numerous requests had been made for the story:

"I determined to build a house of these timbers, but in getting this done I obtained new and unexpected views into human nature, especially as expressed in carpenters. I enthusiastically led the boss carpenter and his five neatly dressed and capable assistants out to this pile of logs which they were to shape into a worthy house, a piece of architecture to which they would refer with pride.

"But they did not enthuse. They did not think of me as crazy—they were too astonished to think. With silent amazement they gazed at these blackened, rough logs. To me their silence was not eloquent. Their pride and long formal experience told them they must not lower the dignity of their craft by using scrapped material. All returned to the city on the noon stage.

"Another head carpenter arrived who had been schooled in smooth surfaces and straight lines. He was heroic and endured for nearly two days. A third came; he felt not only degraded, but also that he would be disloyal to the profession by using these unsawed, unsmoothed tree trunks.

"Nearly every carpenter slighted the joints; they thought that in uniting two logs of different sizes and colors with a poor joint they were doing rustic work. The uncouth is neither rustic nor artistic. Many of the better colored and weather-carved logs were ruined. Some ideas had to be sacrificed and numerous compromises were inevitable.

"Before all, save honor, was lost, an old man arrived who saved the structure. He was not a carpenter, but as a young man had been a boss timberman, had used square sets and stulls, in the old Comstock mines. He knew how to handle timbers. Having an imagination he enthused over the possibilities of these sculptured building timbers.

"Little by little the building took on form. We avoided conspicuous craftsmanship. Joints were neither concealed nor emphasized. We mortised, inset and spiked, pinned, bolted, and clamped. There were no frills nor freaks, no striving for effect, and the simple lines produced substantial and pleasing results. We did not follow a carefully thought out plan, but constantly readjusted and experimented. The finished structure was a good combination of the rustic and the artistic. We builded far wiser than we knew.

"Perhaps the split-log stairway was the most striking object in the living room. Its brown, angular, broken-topped newel post, with heavy broken roots, appeared ancient and substantial. The steps of split logs, banisters of brown, smooth poles, and the spindles of rough, dwarfed timberline trees, all united without a jarring note. These small trees were carried three miles down the mountain on the back of the timberman-artist. The newel posts, though not so aged as some of the timber, had been killed in a forest fire of 1781. Many fire-carved, fire-colored, round timbers—columns—were used in the living room to support the beams of the ceiling. Most of these were varying shades of brown.

"One day after the force had become interested, we asked all to drop tools and follow us into the woods. Two miles away we arrived at a gigantic, upturned tree root. It was about twelve feet in diameter and all agreed that it much resembled a spider web. But it was sound, and its interlaced roots gave an open, artistic screen effect.

"We sat down and discussed it with interest. All heard with astonishment that it was to have a place in the living room. It was too fragile to stand hauling. With care and enthusiasm all hands carried it home. It was placed near a window where it projected webs of shadow upon the floor. This 'spider web screen,' the stairway, the score of tree columns, the rustic furniture grouped in one room were effective. It was primeval—the heart of the ancient wood, and suggested restful forest aisles.

"There were two rough stone fireplaces—not too rough. The stones used were the smoothest that we could find among the broken masses of granite cliffs. These stones showed the chemical stains of time and carried decorative touches of lichen colorings. One fireplace was like a broken ledge of a square-footed cliff; the other had a mantel of granite and on each side two heavy, deeply fire-carved log columns.

"A waste basket made of small poles resembled a log cabin with the roof left off. Injured trees with bent or curved limbs furnished material for chair arms, settee backs, and rockers. A rustic chair that I had made out of small poles sat on my front porch for three or four years. It was not only a comfortable rocker of simple design, but it attracted much attention.

"One day an Eastern woman called to see me. She had shown me many kindnesses, and on departing I asked if I might give her a present. She gleefully went to the rustic chair on the porch. I do not know how much she paid to get it to New England, but three or four of her friends have written me for duplicates. Two poles that had grown with just the right curve formed the rockers, and another furnished the arms.

"Most of the furniture was made of pine and spruce, although aspen was used for a child's high chair. Neither paint nor stain was used. A clear, light, invisible oil was applied to the spruce flooring, and clear shellac made a transparent enamel on the polished table tops.

"Outwardly the structure was substantial and unobtrusive. It did not frighten the peaks and scenery of the nearby mountains. Slightly totem pole effects, with most of the outer logs standing vertical, had here and there a corner post piercing the roof line. The subdued rock or granite color harmonized with the tones of the surroundings. Both the lines and color of this structure allowed it to stand in the little high mountain valley, as though it were a cliff that had been shaped by the same slow acting elemental forces that had shaped the region."

The first meal was served in the new dining-room the Fourth of July, a month after the old building had burned. Work went on throughout the summer, for there were some twenty bedrooms on the second floor to be finished and furnished, but guests were taken care of, even better than before. The abundance of windows was a striking improvement, allowing manifold views of the mountain scenery. In many respects, Mills felt the fire had not been so bad, after all. It had made it necessary for him to start from the beginning, on his own improved plan.

One day a man drove up in a hurry, and Mills met him at the steps, as was his custom with arriving guests.

"I've been told you have some fine scenery up here," the man remarked. "Where is it?" as his indifferent glance took in the landscape.

"I think you have been misinformed," Mills answered.

Mills found some time for guiding this summer, in spite of the heavy demands of the building and the increasing burden of his correspondence. Carl Piltz, who built the fireplace, occasionally helped out with the Peak trips. But Mills foresaw that it would be a serious detriment to the smooth running of the hotel machinery for him to be away all day with parties, and began to look for someone else to take over the guiding.

He selected Shep Husted.

Husted came to the Inn in 1907 and for three summers did most of the guiding on Long's Peak, and working on the trail. Mr. Husted was a born guide, and adept at taking care of parties on the trail and infected everyone with his love of the mountains. Naturally, he absorbed many of Mills's nature guiding principles—putting natural history facts into everyday language—and he never tired of answering questions, an important quality for a guide. Mills trained many guides in the years to follow, and frequently trained his guests for the trip in advance. Even in these later years, he frequently asked Shep Husted or Warren Rutledge to come up from the Park for the Peak trip, always urging inexperienced climbers to take a guide, not only for the factor of safety involved, but for the additional pleasure which they would enjoy.

Mills was not content with having a house full of guests; even though they might be satisfied to look at the scenery from a distance, feeling that they were really very close to the mountains. In one way or another, he would get them out on the trails, send them to timberline to see the alpine flowers, or at least to the "Cascades" where they might hear a water ouzel. And there were always the nearby groves of aspen and pine, flower meadows, and mountain brooks where they could hear "all the songs that wild Nature sings."

To encourage these outdoor interests, rather than have the uninitiated killing time, he asked his guests not to play cards in the lobby. Most of his guests had come for the quiet and the peaceful surroundings of Nature and did not want to be asked to join in a game. For the same reason he did not have a piano, although fond of good music. It was the music of Nature that was cultivated here, the love of her voice, as of her appearance and her life. Naturally, these unusual customs gave the village people something to talk about—"At the Inn there is no music, dancing, or card playing."

If it happened to be a rainy season, which does occur, Mills nevertheless urged people to go outdoors; a rainy day in raincoat and boots was interesting, for one saw many exhibits of Nature not seen on sunny days. And he encouraged people to go off alone, if they did not have congenial company, so they might feel more completely the spell of the wilderness— when there were no distracting influences or inharmonious conversations. And what surprised them even more, he

Enos guiding women on Long's Peak.

suggested a walk at night, even a dark night, affirming not only that night air was healthy, but the wilderness safe and friendly at all times.

If people became lost, he never complained at having to send out rescue parties. He knew the adventure had been worthwhile for the lost; they would not starve, and unless they became panic-stricken would not be apt to suffer serious hardship. In fact, he found they usually came back the happier for the experience. He was always ready to map out trails and routs to distant points and help the tenderfoot with suggestions. He knew the essentials for a successful trip, but he seldom gave advice, unless it was asked, and then not more than he felt would be accepted.

Often there were marshmallow roasts after dinner around a big bonfire in the yard, or perhaps supper would be served under the trees from a stone cook-stove, followed by a quiet walk to one of the beaver ponds to watch the swimmers in the twilight. Throughout the years, several times a week, he would take a carload of guests to one of the more remote beaver colonies, to explain the house building and tree cutting, as well as pointing out many other things along the way—a glaciated boulder, a Calypso orchid, a double-topped tree, or the work of a porcupine—things most would have missed if attention had not been called to them. And sometimes there was a romantic walk by a party of thirty or forty through the moonlit grove, when silence would unconsciously reign; frequently he announced, as the party began to scatter, "If we lose anyone, we won't look for you."

Eventually, after repeated requests, he began giving his nature talks of an evening. They were informal in character, touched the life close at hand, and awakened everyone to the possibility of seeing a bear, finding the first blue-fringed gentian of the season, or hearing the Townsend solitaire. These talks were usually followed by evenings of questions, as Mills moved among his guests: "where did the chipmunks store their peanuts?" "What was the gray bird that wanted part of my lunch?" "Are bears dangerous?" and the seemingly universal one, "Are you snowed-in in winter?" To all of these he gave detailed and enthusiastic answers, for he was in his element when advancing these freshly aroused nature interests.

He often closed his talks with a bit of verse, such as Sam Walter Foss's "The Bloodless Sportsman":

> "I go a-gunning, but take no gun;
> I fish without a pole;
> And I bag good game and catch such fish
> As suit a sportsman's soul;
> For the choicest game that the forest holds,
> And the best fish of the brook,
> Are never brought down by the rifle shot
> And never are caught with a hook.
>
> "I bob for fish by the forest brook,
> I hunt for game in the trees,
> For bigger birds than wing the air
> Or fish that swim the seas.
> A rodless Walton of the brooks
> A bloodless sportsman, I—
> I hunt for the thoughts that throng the woods
> The dreams that haunt the sky.
>
> "The woods were made for the hunters of dreams,
> The brooks for the fishers of song;
> To the hunters who hunt for the gunless game
> The streams and the woods belong.
> There are thoughts that moan from the soul of the pine
> And the thoughts in a bell-flower curled;
> And thoughts that are blown with the scent of the fern
> Are as new and as old as the world.

"So away! for the hunt in the fern-scented wood
  Till the going down of the sun;
There is plenty of game still left in the woods
  For the hunter who has no gun.
So, away! for the fish in the moss-bordered brook
  That flows through the velvety sod;
There are plenty of fish still left in the streams
  For the angler who has no rod."

In 1908, Mills opened Timberline Cabin, the halfway house on the Long's Peak Trail, where food and shelter were obtainable by those desiring to make a two day trip of the climb or who wished to see the sunrise from timberline or explore alpine meadows. For seventeen years this cabin proved a life saver to many an exhausted mountaineer, and a mecca for many a seasoned explorer. Strategically located for scenery and ease of access to many points of interest, it offered the essentials of civilization with a chance at roughing it, which has a charm all its own. Through its telephone connections with Long's Peak Inn, it became the center of most of the rescue work in the surrounding country, and occasionally resembled a hospital ward, with the attendant doing duty as nurse, cook, wood-chopper, and horse-wrangler.

Enos outside Long's Peak Inn.

Such was Mills's confidence in the region, and so hearty the response of his guests, that he continued to enlarge and improve the Inn, although already heavily in debt. In 1908 he built a fine, ten room log cabin called the Forest House, the rooms bearing tree names—Pine, Spruce, Hemlock, Fir, etc. The next year he built an attractive three room cabin for himself in the same artistic, rustic style. This became his 'work-room' the remainder of his life. The little homestead cabin had served his needs well, there was doubtless a pang of regret in leaving it, but he must now be on the Inn grounds, nearer his growing establishment.

In every way Mills devoted himself to the interests of his guests, not overlooking the creature comforts in his enthusiasm for furthering their outdoor activities. Although his own requirements were simple in the extreme, he nevertheless realized that city life made roughing it less and less practical for the majority. He soon met even the growing demands for private bath and steam heat, yet always kept some of the simpler rooms for those of moderate means.

He personally supervised the cooking, that the meals might be well balanced, and the health of his guests kept up to the par which mountain climbing demanded. Simplicity was the keynote, yet care was taken in getting the best grades of food, and seeing that these were properly cooked. He originated a trail lunch which would satisfy, without disastrous results, healthy mountain appetites; substituting jam for ham in the sandwiches, and including an orange, cake of chocolate, and raisins. Raisins he considered the most complete ration for restoring energy quickly, and prevailed upon a national raisin concern to pack these in handy, individual packages.

We find a newspaper clipping of 1913 the favorable impression which this up-to-date mountain inn made on visitors:

"There is a great big hospitable porch, a unique staircase, a curious little post office and a big cheerful dining room. Around about are the dozen or more log cabins of similar style. Some of the "cabins" have as many as ten rooms and one even has city style baths and steam heat—probably reserved for Boston people... With all this goes a dining room service equal to any first class city hotel—better than that—equal in fact to the old farmhouse dinner fare, for on the place is produced the milk, cream, butter, chickens, eggs, and vegetables that satisfy so well your Estes Park appetite."

And another guest remarks: "The rustic idea is carried out in every detail. Not a piece of 'store furniture' is to be seen. The beds, the tables, the chairs, are all made of boards and logs. Even the pincushions are latticed around with sticks...The most interesting features of the Inn are the chipmunks and Mr. Enos Mills, the proprietor. The former are tame and eat peanuts from one's hand or pocket. The latter will give one all the information one can absorb about the mountains of this great Western country."

A delightful description of the Inn appeared in "The Craftsman" for May, 1911, by M. Kennedy Bailey, who said:

"Only a man who is an artist, forest-schooled, could have built these houses and retained, in every line and curve, every angle and bent, the forest idea of harmony that is achieved from infinite variety. Such architecture as this must have been felt before it was conceived... The Master of the House, as his friends delight to call him...demonstrated at every turn his own respect for Nature's handiwork. He succeeded in using rejected material in a manner to convince even the artificially trained eye of its genuine artistic quality. From that it is an easy step to the gospel of the unplucked flower, the wild creature, that, unfrightened, takes you farther than you could otherwise go into the companionship of Nature. 'The Wilds Without Firearms' has become a slogan at Long's Peak, and the world, which seems to be finding a pathway to his door, must inevitably learn to constitute itself a protector of everything wild, be it bird or beast or flower."

One sad incident of 1910 was the death of Mills's faithful dog Scotch, his companion of eight years. Scotch had been trained to put out forest fires, and when he saw a smoking fuse, which the road-men had set, he rushed to extinguish it, losing his life. He had become so much a part of the life at the Inn, accompanying climbers on the trail or entertaining them with games of football with Mills, that he was much missed by everyone. Scotch had grown up with the chipmunks and rabbits around the yard and lived in perfect harmony with them. But this was not true of the strange dogs that came to the place, and Mills eventually refused to take in a guest who brought along a dog.

Like some of the other unwritten laws of the place, this was often hard to enforce. But the chipmunks, rabbits, and birds, as well as the wild flowers, were among the interesting and helpful influences of Nature which Mills wanted his guests to enjoy, and he protected them at any cost. It is said that a Chicago multi-millionaire arrived one day with his dogs, but was given no chance to unpack. Guns were another non-essential not tolerated on his premises.

The work on the Long's Peak Trail was continued through these years and those to follow, chiefly through Mills's efforts, and the road from Estes Park was improved to make it easier for horses. There was still little travel from the south, through Allenspark, but a highway would come in time, for good roads were one of the major projects for which Mills worked in the development of the wilderness. Trails to the scenic attractions were even of more importance, and he urged the usefulness of a continuous trail along the extensive timberline, where magnificent views would be obtained and where the picturesque trees and alpine flowers were at their best.

An automobile stage line had been established between Estes Park and Loveland in 1907 and another over the Lyons road in 1909. These immediately increased the travel and resident population of Estes Park. The replacement of the old Western stage line by the automobile brought forth bitter protest at first, as eliminating a feature of the good enough old days which settlers did not like to see pass out of existence, but the efficiency of the automobile as compared with horses forced the change.

Estes Park had had its greatest impetus in the way of development in the coming of Mr. F. O. Stanley a few years before. In 1908 he built a beautiful hotel at the eastern entrance of the town with a magnificent outlook on Long's Peak and the Continental Divide. This handsome modern hotel, colonial in architecture, was electrically equipped throughout, including kitchen and laundry.

The Estes Park Protective and Improvement Association had been formed in 1906, with Mr. Stanley as president and Mr. C. H. Bond as secretary. Mr. Stanley gives Mr. F. W. Crocker the distinction of having first suggested the importance of this organization. As a direct result of its activities, a fish hatchery—which has placed millions of young trout in the local streams—was built and maintained, and the High Line Drive and the Prospect Mountain and Deer Mountain Trails were constructed. The Association also fostered a sentiment for the protection of big wild animals, with the resultant increase in the mountain sheep and deer population.

But there was still considerable destruction of the forests and wild flowers. The original industries of the region were cattle raising and lumbering. Much of this was now being carried on under leases granted by the Forest Service. The Long's Peak Trail was being despoiled and flowers irretrievably ruined by this ruthless grazing. That these scenes were of more value as tourist playgrounds than as pasture for cattle could not be appreciated by many of Mills's neighbors. Mills endeavored to have some of these leases revoked or restricted, but the Forest Service was obdurate. Their policy was only concerned with economic uses of the public domain. Mills's continued agitation to have the scenery around Long's Peak and Estes Park reserved for its inspirational benefits to humanity brought upon him first the ridicule, then the bitter antagonism, of many of the adjoining homesteaders and settlers.

For more than ten years he was never entirely free from intrigue, spite schemes, and personal vilification. Cattle were run on his premises at night, waterlines cut when a house full of guests would be the most inconvenienced, strikes instigated among his help, and repeated dinner orders given by telephone for large parties that never arrived.

Perhaps one of the main instigators of this trouble was a man of whom Mills had borrowed money giving in return a mortgage on the Inn. As the time neared for payment, this man bragged that he was going to foreclose without warning. A friend got the word to Mills just in time to enable him to pay off the debt and save his property. But the neighborhood feeling of animosity endured.

The sad fate of a mountain sheep a few years before had something to do with Mills's dislike of barbed wire fences. One February a number of sheep were grazing in the meadow near the Inn when a passing team startled them and caused them to dash over the fence and across the road. Three cleared the fence without harm, but the fourth, which had lingered to take in the cause of the disturbance, dashed into the fence, entangling his horns in the wire. In his mad efforts to free himself, he cut his jugular vein and bled to death. This head was preserved by Mills, his one and only trophy of the kind.

Unfenced scenes were more in harmony with Mills's policies; pasture for his stock was enclosed, but the major portion of his extensive acres was left open for the use of the public. That campers, with their careless fires and hacking of trees, did much damage there is no doubt; but the greatest destruction was to the flowers, where trespassing stock grazed and trampled the perishable beauty.

One of the tactics of the neighboring cattlemen was to keep a watchman on guard with a spyglass, and whenever Mills left the place, word was sent around to the neighborhood. On several occasions, after starting northward on horseback, Mills would return unexpectedly and meet cattle being driven upon the Inn grounds.

He continued to find time for writing in addition to the multiplicity of Inn duties and the various troubles incident to its operation. He often used the hours after midnight for completing a story, for which he had jotted down notes between the calls of visitors or the rush of telephone calls. It had become necessary, some years before, to build a private telephone line between Estes Park and the Inn—only one of the many expenditures which made deep inroads on his summers' receipts—since it was important to him to keep in touch with the outside world, meet guests in Estes Park unexpectedly, or order supplies from a distance. A post office had been established at Long's Peak Inn in 1909, and for many years Mills assumed its responsibilities with the routine details involved.

The man's daily activities are concisely summed up in a comment of one of the guests, Mr. Henry M. Wolf, of Chicago, himself a strenuous lawyer, able to appreciate Mills's tremendous energy:

"I was sitting in the reference room taking my first lesson in botany, but in my study could not help but notice what was going on around me. Mr. Mills came into the living room, stopped a moment at the desk, then answered a telephone call, stepped out to greet some new arrivals, answered another telephone call, put a log on the fire, stepped out to the kitchen, was back again to speak to some strangers, answered the telephone, and then went down to the post office. I was reminded of the following anecdote:

"Richard Mansfield was due in Omaha for a one night's performance, and on leaving Chicago sent the following wire:

"'Will arrive Omaha Monday morning. Have the stage manager, the scene shifter, the costume designer, the playwright, and the critic, meet me at the theater at eleven o'clock.'

"Immediately he received this reply from the manager, "'I'll be there.'"

But this was only half the picture. Although Mills sat up with his guests until the last had exhausted all possible subjects of conversation, he was awake with the first of his staff the next morning. He made the rounds of all departments, from cooks to carpenters, taking orders for supplies needed, giving instructions for the day, and developing an understanding of their various problems, so necessary for complete cooperation. His staff were devoted to him, and many returned year after year. His definite policies were sometimes hard to impress upon newcomers, who would not believe that they were to be taken seriously. Mrs. Walden, the head cook for many years, tells of a new pastry cook who put flour in the berry pies, contrary to orders. Mills was always in the dining room promptly, and, after sampling the pies, made a hurried trip to the kitchen. He told the cook her pies were excellent according to the ordinary standards, but in the future she must omit the flour—a nonessential according to his standards, and spoiling the natural flavor of the fruit.

There are not many who would have gone to the trouble of following up these little niceties that make for perfection. But it was this persistent devotion to detail which made the Inn appreciated by everyone who knew it. Mills had an enviable reputation among hotel men, even if they wondered why its proprietor was not content with one line of endeavor. But to Mills, the hotel was chiefly a means off getting people into the wilderness, and he ran it with the same careful attention he gave to all his activities.

Mills had tendered his resignation as salaried lecturer for the Forest Service, to take effect in May, 1908. He had devoted himself to the cause of awakening a public interest in forests, emphasizing their higher values. Now a new need had impressed him as of even greater importance. Before he had reached his fortieth year he started on what he afterward called "the most stimulating and growth compelling" activity of his life. And he did this without any diminution in other lines of work, because these interests all converged in one big field—the outdoors. Mills continued nature guiding throughout his life, even though at times he seemed a prophet without honor in his own country.

Writing and Speaking

"This is a beautiful world, and all who go out under the open sky will feel the gentle, kindly influences of Nature and hear her good tidings. Beauty, like a friend, inspires every one to do his best."
Enos A. Mills

Some fifteen years after his first fruitless efforts at writing, Mills said: "I ever wanted to be a writer. Whatever success I may have had, I think is due to an intense enthusiasm for my subject, a deep interest in Nature, and an unusual array of material about which to write. Much of my best has been written in support of a noble cause."

During his mining days at Butte, Mills became acquainted with Lieutenant E. S. Paxson, the painter of Indians, buffalo herds, and Western life. In addition to being a self-made artist made famous by his picture, "Custer's Last Battle," he was a frontiersman of the most vivid and adventurous type. A character to elicit Mills's admiration, he was the subject of his article, "A Western Artist." This appeared in "Outdoor Life," the best Western magazine of the day, in 1902, and probably was Mills's first magazine contribution.

What other articles may have been printed about this time is unknown, but Samuel Bowles gives a good impression of the name Mills was making for himself, in the "Springfield Republican," August, 1904:

"One of the most interesting men in all Colorado is Enos A. Mills, scientist, journalist, mountaineer, well known to many summer tourists as the Long's Peak guide. His mountain climbing has not been confined to the Peak and its neighborhood. He has roamed all through the northwestern Rockies, and has tramped among the Alps, but the great ranges of Colorado are his special field, and he knows them better than many a man knows his own back yard...Besides nerve, he possesses the faculty of finding his way anywhere, the ability to go straight through woods and over rocks to any point he may have in mind. This, he says, is not acquired, but an instinct which is born in him. And his accurate knowledge of the birds and beasts and rocks and flowers is wonderful, a knowledge not gained in schools, but gathered by long and tireless self-instruction. By the same means he has acquired the ability to write with ease and beauty of expression."

In December, 1904, two articles were accepted by Eastern publications: "Dangers of Snow-Slides" by "Harper's Weekly," and "In the Mountain Snows" by "Youth's Companion." Other articles were to follow in "Youth's Companion," one in 1905 on "The Return Horse"—an account of the special trained ability of mountain horses to return to their stables after being ridden to the top of mountain passes and released by their riders. Most mountain mines were several thousand feet above the towns, and while the miners did not mind walking down, it was a laborious task to climb to their work each morning. Hence the use of "return horses" became the practice, and it was a penitentiary offense to catch one of these horses after its rider had started it homeward.

Another story of typical Colorado animal life, "All about the Wonderful Little Animal—the Burro," was published in "Physical Culture," April, 1905.

The impersonal angle which Mills takes in his writing is very marked. If he had enlarged upon his own exploits, and his contacts both with Nature and with people, it would not have taken the world so long to discover this new type of Western hero. But one almost has to read between the lines, so carefully has he concealed himself in his desire to bring new subjects of interest to his reader, if one is to realize the scope of his achievements.

He early called attention to "The Beauties of Estes Park" as an article in the "Loveland Reporter," 1902, so entitled, reveals. During 1904 and 1905 some ten or twelve lengthy articles on Colorado forests and scenery, with his own photographs, appeared in the "Denver Times Magazine" section and the "Denver Republican." That an immense amount of work went into these articles, and that Mills was writing and revising incessantly, there is no doubt.

At the age of thirty-five, 1905, Mills issued privately his first book, "The Story of Estes Park and a Guidebook," which met an eager demand and ready sale. The first edition was printed by Outdoor Life Publishing Company. It was inscribed to his friend, Robert W. Johnson. The book was revised and re-printed in 1911, 1914, and 1917, and ultimately published with additional material by Houghton Mifflin Company, in 1924, under the title "The Rocky Mountain National Park."

It was the story of the upbuilding of a mountain community, the lives of those who had taken part in its advancement, and the efforts that had been made to preserve the wild life and natural beauty of its magnificent scenes. Mills had been collecting data on the local history for a number of years, interviewing the old pioneers, from the Estes family on down, to learn of their early experiences. But even with the best sources of information to draw upon, memories were not always accurate, and equally authoritative opinions frequently differed. It took much corroborating of dates and incidents, of elimination of prejudices and personal jealousies, to complete the story.

Along with his writing—and the hotel, which occupied his summers—Mills was occasionally speaking in public. Many forestry addresses had been made throughout Colorado, and a few even outside the State, prior to 1905.

But in March, 1905, he made an important talk before the Denver Chamber of Commerce. The local papers were full of encomiums, the "Republican" stating: "The address was one of the most interesting ever delivered before the Chamber and was very well received."

Even more to the point is the fact that a request was made to have the talk printed in its entirety, with the results that it was distributed as an arbor day souvenir among the schools and conservation associations of the State.

J. A. McGuire, of "Outdoor Life," credits this talk as starting Mills's career as a speaker, and declares also that it impressed him as the finest appeal for conservation he ever heard. Incidentally, it came as a complete surprise to him, although he had known Mills for many years, both in Denver and at Long's Peak. Fourteen years after the talk he gave his recollections of it:

"Mills said he wanted to consult me about it. I should have felt pretty nervous to have to deliver a talk before the Chamber of Commerce at that time, so I felt sorry for Mills. I said to him, 'Let's take a walk and talk it over.' My first thought was to try to dissuade him from attempting a speech; for, to be frank, I never thought he would get farther than the introductory sentence. I learned during a conversation that he had written his lecture, but had not attempted to commit it memory, although he had made notes of his chief topics on a card. This partly reassured me...When the day for the lecture arrived, Mills was introduced by President J. S. Temple. There was a large audience. I was on the platform and, feeling a sort of sponsorship for his appearance, held my breath. Mills never believed in dressing up for any function, so on this occasion, like a sturdy oak among other trees, he stood up, garbed in his ordinary clothing of the hills.

("Let me add here that many years later, when he was engaged to speak to a fashionable audience in Philadelphia, he was sent word at the last moment that he could be expected to appear in a dress suit. His reply was sent by a Negro waiter, attired in evening dress, with this note, 'Here's the full dress; I will be unable to attend.')

"Well, at this first lecture in Denver, Mills got through the introductory sentence, that I had dreaded, and before long was talking so fluently and entertainingly that I found myself carried away with him to the timbered summits of his snowy range. His voice seemed a little hoarse at times, as he emphasized some remark, but it wasn't long before he found himself in a manner that surprised and delighted me. He related some witticisms connected with his hill life. One of these was concerned with a day's trip through the mountains to the westward of Long's Peak.

"Noticing a very tall pine which should afford a fine view, he climbed it. When he reached a big limb near the top, he sat down to rest and look about. After a few moments he heard someone approaching through the timber growth, and a conversation between two men who were running in his direction.

"'Yes,' one of the men was saying, 'it's a bear—a small black one.'

"Mills said he let out whoops that could be heard in Utah. He made it clear that he was no bear lolling in the primal balcony, then de-treed himself to be congratulated by the hunters on the strength of his voice.

"The description of the silver spruce which Mills told in that speech remains in my memory yet: 'The silver spruce is truly Colorado's most handsome tree. Her beauty of form, her fluffy, silver-tipped robe, her garland of rich brown cones make her the queen of Colorado's wild gardens.'

"And this also I recall: 'People are feeling the call of the wild; they want the wild world beautiful; they want the temple of the gods, bits of forest primeval, the pure and fern-fringed brooks. They like to stand knee-deep in June. They demand the shadows of the pines and have them they will.'

"When Mills told of the death of a woodsman and recluse who lived in the Long's Peak region all his life, his voice dropped almost to a whisper.

"'Enos,' the recluse had once said, 'before I go I want to tell you about the grove of Engelmann spruce above the cabin. You know I've watched and guarded it from danger all my life, and now I want you to take over the trust.'

"I believe the sound of a pin climbing could have been heard as he repeated those words. When he ended his talk I said to him, 'Mills, you have covered yourself with glory.' I was not the only one to congratulate him; there were dozens coming up to clasp his hand."

The demand for lecture dates came from all corners of the State, due to the enthusiasm of his audience and the appealing information disseminated in the printed booklet. He had full command of his subject, and presented it with direct simplicity. And he was heard of in distant states. Early in the autumn of 1905, Mills commenced a forestry lecture tour of the East, speaking in Kansas City, Memphis, New Orleans, Pittsburgh, Columbus, and Chicago, among the many cities visited, making about eighty addresses, all at his own expense.

On many of his early lecture trips he carried a lantern and slides made from his own pictures, but he soon gave this up. He found that the pictures distracted the attention of the audience; they sat back and enjoyed the magnificent scenes thrown on the screen, and lost much of what he was saying. He wanted people to get his facts and his feeling for the forests, and start working to help save them.

He was back in Colorado briefly, in December, 1905, for he had promised Mrs. George Packard, of Denver, to give a talk before her Art and History Club. Mrs. Packard had known him only as a reticent and rather silent mountaineer and had never heard him speak in public. But she wanted to assure him an audience and had invited everyone she knew. Then, as everyone came, she began to dread a fiasco. Like McGuire, she began to worry lest her lecturer might not be equal to the occasion.

The meeting was held in the hall and living-room of her home, the stairs being used to seat the overflowing audience. Just as Mills began to speak, there was a clatter and then a scream. A lady trying to find a place on an upper step tripped and hurtled downward, upsetting others on the way. "This," thought Mrs. Packard in despair, "will certainly finish him."

But Mills had no notion of being troubled. He waited till the hubbub ceased and then continued as if falling ladies were no more disquieting than falling stars. He started talking immediately on his subject—"Colorado Forests"—with no preliminary remarks, and spoke with that simple eloquence and ardor that made him in time one of the country's best liked public speakers. When he had finished and been mildly applauded, he asked if there were any questions. Again Mrs. Packard had a qualm; he knew his speech, but with how would he conduct himself in making unprepared replies, she wondered.

She need not have worried. When one of the ladies asked whether it was true that only one species of tree was safe to take shelter under from lightning in a thunderstorm, he replied, "The safest thing is always to be prepared to die, then it won't matter what tree you stand under."

But if Enos was finding trees a popular subject to talk and write about, he himself was furnishing much news material for other writers. His unique life in the mountains, his independence of thought and work, his intense devotion to the cause of the outdoors, and his deep interest in what others were doing a long conservation lines, combined to make him a man whom everyone was glad to hear about.

Among the interesting news items was won by a Mila Tuppard Maynard in the "Denver News-Times Illustrated Weekly," March, 1906:

"During the winter just closing, Mr. Mills has spoken before three state forestry associations, eight universities, several boards of trade, and clubs innumerable—this gratuitous and valuable aid should be appreciated and better understood by the people of the State, for that such efforts are a tremendous economic as well as sentimental importance, a moment's thought will readily show.

"Colorado has produced a number of unique personalities born of her fertile mountains and tonic freshness. One of these is Enos A. Mills, lecturer on forestry and forest preservation, former state snow inspector, for many years a guide, especially for the climbing of Long's Peak, and proprietor of Long's Peak Inn above Estes Park.

"Mr. Mills has done the State so large a service and

promises to continue that service so effectively that it is time Colorado people knew more of the man and his unusual realm of enthusiasm and knowledge.

"During the past year this lover of the trees has, without any recompense and at considerable expense, traveled thousands of miles in a half-dozen different states to speak on forest preservation and forest development. The man's earnestness and sincerity have made his work remarkably effective in spreading information regarding that great problem of saving the world's timber supply and an arousing enthusiastic, organized cooperation in the forestry movement.

"Next week he speaks again in Denver and in June before the Federation of Women's Clubs in St. Paul. The National Department of Forestry has frequently expressed its appreciation of his cooperation and recognized the extent and thoroughness of his knowledge of this subject. And now that the times are ripe to give a hearing to this question, it is fortunate that a personality so refreshing, from a region so full of charm and marvel, with an experience so broad in his familiarity with all the majesty of the Colorado heights, should be the messenger to carry the needed word."

The tour which he embarked on early in 1906 carried him from Colorado to Butte, Montana, and ended at St. Paul, Minnesota, June 4, with a talk on "The Forest" at the Biennial Convention of the General Federation of Woman's Clubs. The "Rocky Mountains News," Denver, gave the general verdict:

"After everybody was tired out...there arose a man who looked as though he had blown in from the field, a man with a retiring manner and halting attitude. But when that man had uttered a sentence, the Federation rubbed its eyes, ran its fingers through its crimps, perked up its ears, shook off its tired feeling, and for 30 minutes listened to such poetry of trees, running brooks, white, silent places of nature, the songs of birds and the great world lessons in the deep forests, from the lips of a man who spoke straight from his heart to the heart of every woman present. And after it was all over, Enos A. Mills, the state snow observer, who spent his life studying and loving the trees and all Nature, was declared the success of the Federation. At the conclusion of his address Mr. Mills was given an ovation."

The St. Paul papers, too, were full of favorable comment. The "Daily Dispatch" said:

"It was borne in upon today's audience that convention speakers are yet to be like birds in that those of finest plumage and most showy manners do not excel in the quality of their singing.

"Mr. Mills was the first speaker to demonstrate the truth of this. He looks like a modest woodsman, eager-eyed and keen to know the beauty that lies in the heart of things...His hands wear the look of contact with the things of the forest; he is lithe and quick rather than dignified. But in his speech he is glowing and earnest, his voice good and his English smooth and flowing. Before he had finished you were convinced that his slim alertness, high brow and searching eyes exactly fitted, while they did not burden, the great message he had to convey. Mr. Mills has been the particular hit of the Convention."

The influence of this address, in reaching the public-spirited women of the country, can hardly be estimated. Before he left the Convention he received appeals from various enthusiastic members, asking for more of the message so new to them. A characteristic one was:

"MY DEAR MR. MILLS:
"I know you will excuse the voice from Louisiana that tells you that you have touched my heart with your forest voice. Can I have your address? I want you to tell me where I can get a copy of your beautiful 'Tree Truths.' I send you a cordial handclasp, heartfelt. Thanks.
"(Mrs.) FRANCES SHUTTLEWORTH."

Mrs. Shuttleworth succeeded in having Mills speak before the Louisiana State Federation, and for years directed the forest conservation work in her State. Always she hoped to visit Colorado, never forgetting the inspiring words of the Colorado naturalist in defense of the forests. Her hope was realized in 1933, when she visited the Inn and told Mrs. Mills of memory of that talk in 1906 when Mr. Mills had given his message to the General Federation.

During the summer of 1906, Mills was dated for more than fifty addresses, and started in October on a tour that took him from Pueblo, Colorado, to Boston. Among the many cities included in the tour were Portsmouth and Dayton, Ohio, Chicago, Peabody, Massachusetts, and Saratoga, New York. These were the first addresses for which he received remuneration. And in addition to the paid talks, he made about an equal number of gratuitous talks.

He suited his talks to the occasion and the audience, nor did he hesitate to use names. At the Twentieth Century Club in Boston, November, 1906, an audience of the seriously cultured of that most cultured of American cities, and presided over by Bliss Perry, editor of the "Atlantic Monthly," he spoke of the immediate dangers to American forests, declaring:

"A Bill has been before Congress for years to preserve the White Mountains and Appalachian forests and add them to the national forest reserves, and one man only has prevented its passage. That man is Speaker Cannon, who also prevents the preservation of the Big Trees of California. You can save them if you will express yourselves."

Mills took occasion on these eastern trips to visit to forests and notable scenery of other states. His interest was not alone in his own Colorado. As Allen Chamberlain said in the "Boston Transcript":

"It has been said that Mills is doing for the Rockies what Muir did for the Sierra Nevada Mountains. This is unjust to both men, for it never was in either of them to be sectional. One has but to listen to Mills to realize his unselfishness and nationwide interest. He is, for example, as eager as any Yankee to see our New England White Mountains protected as a national forest, and for the promotion of this he has done his part. Mills is the prophet from the Rockies, not, as he has sometimes been called, the prophet of the Rockies. He carries to the stay-at-home public the best of what Muir calls the mountains' 'good tidings.'"

Mills was asked by the governor of Massachusetts to accept the post of state forester, but declined.

His field was as wide and unlimited as the outdoors itself, and his interest covered every phase of Nature. He was on common ground with nature lovers in the East, while being an acknowledged authority on the much less appreciated West. He came to know John Burroughs, a man as simple and direct as himself, and delighted in telling him of the birds and animals of his mountains. He met William Lyman Underwood and saw the little bear cub, later written of in Underwood's book, "Wild Brother." What bear stories the two must have swapped! He came in touch with John M. Phillips, who was leader of the Boy Scout movement in Pittsburgh, as well as a remarkable photographer of wild life. His picture of a mountain goat was used by Mills in the first edition of "Watched by Wild Animals." He had firsthand acquaintance with the work of men like Dr. W. T. Hornaday and Dr. C. Hart Merriam, who were extending the knowledge of wild life, and he enjoyed the work of Mary Austin and those ardent bird lovers, Olive Thorne Miller and Florence Merriam Bailey.

While deeply interested in the work others were doing, Mills's Eastern trips were mainly occupied with his efforts to arouse the general public to his own particular interests. It was before the day of popular nature study and education, and much natural history information was too scientific for the multitude. Mills gave his audience a new interpretation of the outdoors, with his adventure stories, and then left them with something definite to work for, begging every man, woman, and child to help save America's best scenery, its birds, wild life, and forests.

He made the happy acquaintance of Edward Everett Hale, Chaplain to the United States Senate, who appreciated the worth of what Mills was doing and in August 25, 1907, wrote him:

"Tell your people that if they want their children's children to see the United States what the desert countries of Western Asia are—they will cut down the forests for another generation, as they are now doing. The lands of Croesus, the richest of kings are now the abode of jackals, where they cannot find anything to eat, because Croesus and the fools like him did not preserve the forests."

There was in the White House at this time a man to whom the American wilderness was almost as dear as it was to Mills, and who knew the West intimately and loved it, President Theodore Roosevelt. He had been following Mills's tireless and independent educational program, and realized his unusual ability to reach the public. He appreciated the fund of information which the man had at his command, as well as his devoted enthusiasm. Here was the person he needed to help save the country's resources for the future.

President Roosevelt sent for Mills, and the interview which followed only deepened his convictions of the importance of forest conservation. He offered Mills a post as Government Lecturer on Forestry under the Chief Forester, Gifford Pinchot. From January, 1907, until May, 1909, he held this position.

Mills returned to Colorado soon after receiving his appointment to arrange for an extended tour. He had made more than a hundred addresses the preceding fall in the East, and his home State was more eager than ever to hear him. He spoke in Greeley, Colorado Springs, Salida, and before the Chamber of Commerce and the Real Estate Exchange in Denver. But March found him in Tuscola, Illinois, April in Omaha and May in Helena, Montana, addressing the Civic Club, with no knowing how many stops in between.

He continued his lecturing much as formerly, with the added prestige of his new title. But he was as fearless as ever in his condemnation of those who were allowing the forests to be destroyed or neglected through selfish interests or lack of interest.

"I can't tell how I drifted into this field," Mills said when asked about his lecturing; "I suppose I liked it. My life brought me into intimate touch with what might be called the philanthropic side of the forest. My work is this—I want to save the forests."

"Few men would give themselves so wholeheartedly to the cause," the interviewer remarked.

"Now, don't give me too much credit for this," Mills answered. "I am having a lot of fun out of it. This is my life. It isn't as though it were drudgery. It is pure joy."

"What type of audience do you prefer?" was asked.

"Wherever there is genuine interest. The economic side is now appealing to men, where formerly it was hard to get a hearing. I speak in colleges, women's clubs and men's congresses. I talk forestry everywhere I go. Last summer while I was out doing missionary work I went broke. I took a position on a river steamer on the Mississippi River and when I wasn't busy I talked forestry to the passengers. It is wonderful what a man can do by way of educating people when he starts with a purpose."

The fall of 1907 finds him making a tour of Georgia, as a freelance forestry agent. He gave many talks at the forestry meetings held that winter by the Appalachian National Forest Association, in the effort to secure adequate forest legislation for the Appalachian Mountains.

Governor Hoke Smith was in the audience one night when Mills ended on of his serious, appealing talks with his incomparable story of a Thousand Year Pine. Governor Smith was so moved by the story that he insisted Mills accompany him home to repeat it for the benefit of his wife and daughter. Mills was taking an early train the following morning, and nothing would do but that Mrs. Smith and her daughter had to be routed out of bead to hear this marvelous tree epic, and meet the man whose intimate tree knowledge had made possible the deciphering of the tree's story.

And Mills always reached young people. One newspaper comment reads: "He made a nice appeal to the boys and explained why they should protect the birds. He asked one little boy which he would rather have, a sparrow or a worm. The boy did not fancy the worm, but had never had a sparrow. Mills illustrated his point by saying that the birds destroyed the worms, and that the worms if not killed by the birds would destroy the trees. Therefore, the boys were not wise when they killed birds and robbed nests...The talk was full of wholesome advice and did much to impress upon his hearers the value of a systematic effort toward the covering of the mountainsides with growing trees."

Another reporter says: "The boys seriously objected to the length of the talk—it was entirely too short."

While addressing the Chicago Latin School, at the end of the boy's long day, he saw he must get started quickly if he was to catch their attention. The moment he was introduced, he started to speak at a rapid fire rate, walking straight across the platform toward his audience and right off the platform, dropping some four feet below. Without a break in his story, he backed toward the steps and up to the platform again, as though nothing had happened. Every boy's eyes and ears were directed toward the speaker from that moment to the end of the talk.

One of his favorite bears stories was connected with an incident that happened to him in Yellowstone Park. Being known as the "tree climber" by his fellow surveyors, he had been persuaded to climb a tree adjacent to one in which a young bear was lodged, with the instructions to prod the bear down. Sure enough, the bear was dislodged, but the moment it reached the ground it started to climb the tree in which Mills was sitting. When telling this story at Tuskeegee Institute, Alabama, the laugh became so uproarious at this point, and continued for so long, that he could not finish it, and thereafter he never tried to, concluding that the tale had reached a

Enos outside his cabin at Long's Peak Inn, where he wrote many of his stories.

natural climax.

The first decade of the century marked a rapid advance in the forest conservation program of the nation. The American people were becoming conscious of their heritage in scenery, wild animal life, tree and flower; but this awakening was not a spontaneous product, it was the result of continuous efforts of a few public spirited men, among whom Enos Mills had a foremost and active place.

In addition to his lecturing, he was writing nature stories and forestry articles for "Youth's Companion", "Recreation", "Suburban Life", and many other periodicals. "Destruction of Western Forests" appeared in "Outdoors Magazine", January, 1906; "The Beaver and His Works" in "The World Today", December, 1908; and "The Life of a Thousand Year Pine" in "World's Work", for August, 1908. This last, under the title "The

Story of a Thousand Year Pine," has been translated into several foreign languages, transcribed into shorthand and made into braille, and is considered Mills's finest single story. It was included in "Wild Life on the Rockies," and later published as a separate book under its own title.

There were repeated requests for these stories in permanent form, and in March, 1909, Houghton Mifflin Company published "Wild Life on the Rockies." In the Preface, Mills states that it records "a few of the many happy days and novel experiences which I have had in the wilds. For more than twenty years it has been my good fortune to live most of the time with Nature, on the mountains of the West...a nature lover charmed with the birds and trees." The book was most appropriately dedicated to John Muir.

It was like Muir's and Burrough's books, a combination of personal adventure with description and information, without sentimentalizing or moralizing. Written simply and vividly, even the most desk-bound city dweller could follow the adventures described and see the scenes pictured. It had a freshness and eager joy in the out-of-doors that made it attractive and appealing. The book was widely and favorably reviewed, and one of the oft-quoted paragraphs follows:

"I never see a little tree bursting from the earth, peeping confidently up among the withered leavers, without wondering how long it will live or what trials or triumphs it will have. I always hope it will find life worth living, and that it will live long to better and beautify the earth. I hope it will love the blue sky and the white clouds passing by. I trust it will welcome all seasons and ever join merrily in the music, the motion and the movement of the elemental dance with the winds. I hope it will live with rapture in the flower-opening days of spring and also enjoy the quiet summer rain. I hope it will be a home for the birds and hear their low, sweet mating songs. I trust that when comes the golden peace of autumn days, it will be ready with fruited boughs for the life to come. I never fail to hope that if this tree is cut down, it may be used for a flagpole to keep our glorious banner in the blue above, or that it may be built into a cottage where love will abide; or, if it must be burnt, that it will blaze on the hearthstone in a home where children play in the firelight on the floor."

Mills had found himself. It was now a question of finding time to put his experiences and his fund of information into print.

"Country Life" published a series of articles in their "See America" department, and many nature stories were to appear in the "Saturday Evening Post", "Country Gentleman", "Outlook", "Munsey's", "Cosmopolitan", "McClure's", "Sunset", and "Atlantic Monthly" during the next twelve years. Mills often sat up half the night, after finishing the long day's demands at the Inn, to complete some timely article or editorial on conservation of scenery or on national parks. He was giving his best efforts to "some noble cause." In his books he gave his readers the irresistible appeal of the outdoors, hoping to incite them to discover for themselves Nature's boundless gifts for human well being.

In November, 1911, Houghton Mifflin Company brought out "The Spell of the Rockies," a book dealing more largely than any other of Mills's with different aspects of forest life. Mills had real ability to see Nature as a whole, to correlate the life of animals and plants, the relation of trees to streamflow and climate, the constructive forces of geology, and to place each within the realm of human interest and economics. He takes the reader along with him, as one reviewer says:

"To read this book is to climb with the author almost inaccessible heights, to know the spirit of deep forests, to be initiated into much secret lore of mountain, meadow, and wood lore which ought to be the possession of every American."

Mills found time between national park and inn work to bring together his twenty-seven year study of beavers, for his book "In Beaver World," the most comprehensive popular account of the beaver in existence. This, too, was published by Houghton Mifflin Company. It appeared March, 1913, and was heartily received, one comment reading:

"An admirable example of what an 'outdoor book' ought to be; and perhaps more books of the sort would come to us to be admired and remembered if more writers spent years and years of observational study in the woods before they wrote them. This sort of study lies behind the volume, for its author has been a mountain-tramping man all his life. The book is definite and valuable addition to our knowledge of the intellect of this most interesting of animals. Moreover, it is good writing."

Another reviewer says: "With all the millions spent in

saving our forests and streams, we are apt to forget one incorruptible and untiring conservationist who is well worth rewarding with the only price he asks—his life. The valuable public servant is the beaver. His dams and reservoirs are of inestimable value in flood time, and while he uses a great deal of timber for them and his food, he cuts down only such trees as sprout from both stump and roots to renew themselves. He is fascinating to watch, and his habits and methods of work as described by his friend, Enos A. Mills, in the recently published book "In Beaver World" makes most interest reading."

The next year Mills found time to revise "The Story of a Thousand Year Pine" for publication as a separate book. It is used in the reading courses of most elementary schools of the nation, and has been termed a primer on forestry, as well as a classic in tree literature.

In April, 1915, "The Rocky Mountain Wonderland" appeared, with stories of mountain sheep, grizzly bears, lions, chipmunks, birds, and beaver. This book was followed by the publication of "The Story of Scotch" in an edition of its own, 1916.

It is no wonder that Mills's name became a familiar one in the East, and a beloved, if somewhat envied, one in Colorado. Arthur Chapman pays delightful tribute in the "Denver Republican", 1909:

> ENOS MILLS OF ESTES PARK
> Up where Long's Peak stabs the blue,
> Where the night wind hollers through
> All them pine trees—there he writes
> Tales about them magic nights
> In the snowy, wintry hills,
> Where the snowslide roars and kills—
> Writes about the ancient trees
> Till it seems as if the breeze
> Dictates things for him to print—
> Things no breese'd ever hint
> Unto chaps like you and me.
> Durn it all! Why can't we see
> All them wonders of the slopes
> Where our poor blind vision gropes,
> Missin' flowers and sech things,
> Missin' every bird that wings!
> Seems as if that old Long's Peak
> Passed the word along the creek,

Up the gulch and down the draw,
'Long the ridge, jest like a saw,
Where the hills stretch South and North—
Sent a kindly message forth,
Biddin' all the hill-things rise
And show themselves afore his eyes.
That's jes' why this sturdy chap,
Wind-burnt, keen and from his cap
Down to snow-shoed toe and heel
Strong as any piece of steel—
That's why he delights us so,
Writin' things we'd never know.
Shines like campfire in the dark,
Does this Mills of Estes Park!

The thoroughness with which Mills made his observations before publishing his articles can hardly be exaggerated. On one occasion he returned a check which had been sent him for a story on "Twisted Trees," because he said he had not as yet reached a definite explanation of the cause of this twisted condition in some trees. It was a subject which interested him greatly, and he continued to study individual trees to get complete evidence. Many accepted theories were exploded by what he found in examining trees in various sections of the country. At length, however, he did reach a satisfactory explanation—that the twist was caused by the rock-bound obstruction of the circulation in the roots of the tree. His final article was published in "Country Life", January, 1921.

In the same way, he beaver observations were carried ahead by constantly checking his conclusions, before accepting any characteristic as final and absolute. He gave the beaver full credit for marvelous skill in engineering, but he did not give it any credit for sinking its logs in storing the winter food supply; for these green aspen quickly became waterlogged and sank of their own accord, as he learned from experiences once in attempting to cross a stream on a raft of green aspen.

All his fund of information might not have added to the world's storehouse of knowledge if he had not persistently endeavored to learn to write and to speak, and it is interesting to know the books that proved most helpful to him in this study.

William Cobbett, "Grammar of the English Language."
Richard Grant White, "Words and Their Uses; Everyday

English."
    Alfred Holbrook, "A New English Grammar."
    Virginia Waddy, "Elements of Composition and Rhetoric."
    John H. Genung, "Outlines of Rhetoric."
    Frank H. Fenno, "The Science and Art of Elocution."
    George Jacob Holyoake, "Public Speaking and Debate."

Enos at his desk in his cabin at
Long's Peak Inn.

Work for the Nation
"Father of the Rocky Mountain National Park"

"The supreme triumph of Parks is humanity. Nature is universal, and in her ennobling and boundless scenes prejudice, caste, and creed are forgotten. He who feels the spell of the wild, the rhythmic melody of falling water, the echoes among the crags, the bird songs, the wind in the pines, and the endless beat of wave upon the shore, is in tune with the universe, he will know what human brotherhood means."

    Enos A. Mills

In the years that had elapsed since his return from abroad, Mills had spared no efforts in the fall and winter months to carry his plea for forest conservation throughout Colorado and into all the larger cities of the Eastern States. He had awakened general interest, not only in trees, but also in outdoor adventure, mountain climbing, and wildlife protection. More and more, Eastern people were asking where and how to see the magnificent scenes described by him, and how to find those trails to towering, snow-trimmed peaks, quiet, forest-edged lakes, and alpine flower gardens.

At home, Mills was advocating a "Scenic Directory of Colorado," hoping to arouse Coloradoans to see more of their own State. Until they were familiar with the attractions, they could not well direct travelers to them. Millions of dollars were being spent abroad each summer because of the lack of incentive to see more of America. The West was uncharted for the tourists.

The suggestion was a timely one and the "Denver Republican" commented on its wisdom in an editorial, saying:

"Mr. Mills has scored an excellent point. If every citizen made it a rule to acquaint himself with the wonders of his own State, he would turn naturally to others. Companionship with Nature should begin at home. Then once the friendship has been established, it will be carried to the far corners of the earth, but the traveler should first know his own State and then his own country before he sets his face toward foreign shores."

Mills especially urged a more intimate acquaintance with that wild, rugged "roof of the world" that filled the western horizon with lofty landmarks. He suggested the need for a mountain climbing organization to unite the interests and activities of nature loving enthusiasts within the State. He proposed restoring some of the old Indian names to the peaks, mountains, and streams in Colorado, especially around Estes Park, where the recollection of these still lingered.

In his constant work for good roads, he recommended the use of convict labor in the State. This had successfully been tried out in other states—producing not only good roads, but helping to make good citizens of the convicts, the helpful work in healthful scenes being a beneficial influence. He had studied this work at Canyon City, and wrote an article for "Munsey's Magazine," entitled, "The Unguarded Convict." While talking to the men there and gathering data, he was approached by a lady visitor who asked solicitously, "And what are you in for?"

Mills did not like to see opportunities for progress going to waste. Sometimes he would approach a group of his guests, with the comment, "What's up?" and if there was no response, he would add, "Why don't you start something?" Many of his progressive ideas for the public good were taken up and developed by others, but of course some where lost for the want of a leader to carry them through. Once the suggestion was made, he usually went on to new and bigger projects ahead.

Early in 1909 he began on a plan which was to occupy his fullest efforts for the next six years. The need of a national park in Colorado—to put Colorado scenery on the map—had been evident for some time. To have Colorado appreciated at its true worth, it would have to be given a place of importance in the national life. Once the people of the entire country owned this scenic wonderland, had a hand in its administration and development, he felt sure their interest in it, and their use of it, would be enormously increased. The East should meet the West, the city dweller should know the mountains, and out of this broader understanding and sympathy true patriotism would develop. To love one's country, one must know it.

When Mills announced his project to the dwellers in Estes Park, they thought it another one of his dreams. The season had been good, people were coming into the region as fast as they could be comfortably handled, and they could see no reason for a national park.

Mills started eastward with his scheme. As before, he gave talks on adventure and Colorado scenery, stories of trees, birds, bears, and beaver, ending each talk with an appeal for a national park; his platform:

"Around Estes Park, Colorado, are mountain scenes of exceptional beauty and grandeur. In this territory is Long's Peak and one of the most rugged sections of the Continental Divide of the Rockies. The region is almost entirely above the altitude of 7500 feet, and in it are unrivaled forests, streams, waterfalls, snowy peaks, great canyons, glaciers, scores of species of wild birds, and more than a thousand varieties of wild flowers.

"In many respects this section is losing its wild charms. Extensive areas of primeval forests have been misused and ruined, sawmills are humming and cattle are in the wild gardens! The once numerous big game has been hunted out of existence and the picturesque beaver are almost gone.

"These scenes are already extensively used as places of recreation. If they are to be permanently and more extensively used and preserved, it will be necessary to hold them as public property and protect them within a national park."

Lecturing was never a commercial proposition to Mills—it was a campaign for the things he believed in. He might have signed up with a lecture bureau and become a popular, well-paid feature. But he preferred to work as a freelance, going wherever the greatest opportunity afforded. He spoke before commercial organizations, luncheon clubs, colleges, literary and study groups, as well as open meetings in museums and churches, wherever an intelligent, progressive audience was assured. It was not a question how much money he would be paid—but how much attention he would receive.

Often he took time to address school children, finding they were among his most appreciative listeners. In one lecture he said something to the effect that bears would continue to add their interest to the wilderness if we would be good to them. As usual, at the end of the talk he asked if there were any questions. Immediately a little boy asked, "Mr. Mills, what do you do to be good to bears?" Nothing could have delighted him more.

Editors were always glad to get firsthand information on this question of national parks, and newspaper comments were widespread and favorable. Numerous articles under Mills's name appeared in magazines and weeklies, with illustrations of the proposed park, setting forth the attractions of the region.

When Mills returned home, in late winter, the news of his successful campaign had preceded him. Estes Park appeared eager to fall in line, and the Estes National Park and Game Preserve looked assured, but it was not to be won so easily as that. Misleading statements against the advisability of making a national park of the region were being circulated, and the newly-won supporters of the plan quickly stampeded. They were led to believe that their private property would be jeopardized, that Mills himself was working for a position of importance in the new regime, that the whole character of Estes Park would be changed, with a hundred and one other false accusations.

The opposition, both open and under cover, was chiefly engineered by the Forest Service. Most of the territory proposed for the new park was under Forest Service supervision, and was being used under their permits for lumbering and grazing. Naturally, they did not want to relinquish it. The Forest Service, under the Department of Agriculture, controlled an area as large as France; one third of the State of Colorado alone having been set aside in forest reserves. The numerous jobs it provided made a powerful and far-reaching political machine.

In a measure, Mills was prepared for this opposition. He was familiar with the aggressive policies of the Forest Service, and knew of its plan to get control of all the undeveloped scenic areas of the West, under the guise of forestry conservation. The fact that much of the area was unsuited for forestry purposes, being along the most rugged and broken sections of the Continental Divide, much of which was above timberline and contained high peaks and alpine lakes whose only value was their unspoiled beauty, was not considered.

Mills started out in the fall of 1909 on a new attempt to convince the public that the scenes around Estes Park were worthy of preservation. He quoted many authorities on the scenic beauties of the region—Dr. F. V. Hayden, father of the Yellowstone National Park; Horace J. McFarland, of the American Civic Association; Edward Orton, Jr., State Geologist of Ohio; Frederick F. Chapin, of the Appalachian Mountain Club, all of whom had visited the region and pronounced upon its unusual array of attractions for the mountaineer and the vacationist, and had urged the more general use of these ideal realms of natural beauty for rest and enjoyment by the public.

Moreover, the withdrawal of this tract from its present

place in the public domain would do no harm to anyone; most of the area for the proposed national park was between 9000 and 14,000 feet above sealevel, and unavailable for agriculture or mining; while its geographical location, within comparatively easy reach of millions of Eastern people, made it a natural playground for the nation.

Under proper care the forests would flourish, protected from both axe and fire; so, too, would the wildflower gardens—so precariously rooted in shallow, rocky soil, so easily destroyed by the grazing of cattle. As a national park the region would provide for the public a place in which to grow and rest, freedom to camp and linger by the shores of health-giving lakes, in the warm sunshine of hidden dells golden with sunflowers, and along clear streams, with snowy waterfalls, blessed by all the benedictions of Nature.

Newspaper men in Colorado who had a long acquaintance with Mills gave him and the park their unqualified endorsement. One of the more original of these comments was written by Alvin T. Steinel, for the "Fort Collins Evening Courier," February, 1910, and was headed "Our Office Boy Meets an Author":

"I met a real author yesterday...His name is Enos Mills, and besides bein' an author, he is the owner of Long's Peak. He has clumb all over the peak, summer and winter, knows his habits, seen where the wind comes frum, kin read the language of clouds, talk to the birds and beasts on his mountain and he never would harm even a caterpillar that is tryin' to kill a aspen tree, he is that kind to animals. Mills is tryin' to persuade congress to make a national park outen Estes Park, but congress don't think it's good fur us. Ain't it a blessin' that we has a congress to keep us frum makin' serious mistakes that we would regret the rest of our lives? What do we out here know about Estes Park? What do we know about the benefits of havin' it a national park, where you can't shoot game, or hunt beaver with impunity and dynamite? How kind it is of our congress to tell us that we don't know what we want. God bless our congress! Mr. Mills...is kinda queer—all authors is. He does a lot of things for nothin'—a very uncommon trait that is fast dyin' out in our country, because they has been hunted to death. If they passes the national park bill I hope they will put in a clause preservin' Enos, fur the species is gettin' rarer every day. I guess it's nice to be one of the children of nature, but it don't pay very well. Here's luck to Enos; the bears and beavers will thank him if the human beings don't."

Mills made the opportunity to visit John Muir again, with whom he had been in constant correspondence, and Muir heartily applauded Mills's determination to carry his campaign across the nation, assuring him that he would help in every way he could with his pen; but emphasizing the importance of firsthand contact with editors, legislators, and influential members of Congress.

Mills, to save his own time and that of others, interviewed only those whom he knew to be interested in what he had to present. He would have someone sound out the man in advance, to find out if he had an open mind, at least, for the subject to be discussed. He had no difficulty in meeting influential people, who knew of his good work of the past ten years or had read his books, but the important thing was to find those who would champion the good cause, once the need was put before them.

But America lagged far behind Mills. It was easy enough to endorse a movement when it required no personal effort or sacrifice; but to work for it, and that against strenuous opposition, and sometimes brutal denunciation, was a different matter. Many had been silenced by the opposing forces working secretly against the Park, while professing to be for it. Many were confused, as the enemy wanted them to be, by seemingly contradictory statements and actions. Others had been instigated to raise doubts about the importance of the issue; or to suggest that it was not yet time to try to put it through.

Yet little by little, objections were conquered. The bill began to take form. All prior claims of mining, water, and road rights were to be protected. Mills's campaigning took him frequently to Washington, lobbying for the bill, as well as for other measures of vital importance to the cause of conservation. He was non-sectional in his interest—the Grand Canyon or the forests of white pine in Pennsylvania came in for a share of his work, along with the Estes National Park and Game Preserve.

Often he went broke in his determined effort to win the interest of the public, and, through them, to force Congress to respond. Once he took a job of reporting on a New York paper to carry him until he could finish some definite part of his program. On another occasion he was paid to assist a Congressman in composing a speech, and thus replenished his funds.

At times the fight was considered dead and its defeat triumphantly celebrated by the opposition. But the fight was not dead. Even during the busy summer months, when Mills's days and nights were full of hotel duties, he was hammering away. No one can know how many thousands of letters, newspaper articles, and magazine stories were written in defense of the national park project. Numerous were the individuals enlisted to help in the work and from time to time he had vigorous and telling assistance. But he alone remained with it from start to finish; upon him lay the brunt of lecturing, writing, and lobbying for the issue. This took a vast amount of time, energy, and money. He was frequently in debt, and on one occasion had to return to Colorado in the midst of important legislation to negotiate a loan.

In spite of the tremendous battle, Mills did not become bitter. His was a public, not a personal, fight. Many of those who took opposite sides had been friends; they were still friends, though with different views, on the one, to him, all-important question. Many who were using insidious methods to block the park and attacked his character, could, if they choose, look back upon personal favors sought and granted, and unusual acts of kindness, through which they had benefitted at Mills's expense. Campaigning did not change Mills's nature, it simply deepened and broadened it. He once said that the test of all effort should be, not what it gives us, but how deeply it makes us live. He never doubted that he would win in the end, but how long it would take, how much labor it would consume, to these he gave no thought. He had lived too long and intimately amid the great forces of Nature, studied the life of rocks and trees too sympathetically, to be disturbed by human lets and hindrances, or to become ruffled by the difficulties placed in his path.

One winter night one of his active opponents arrived at Mills's cabin in a very penitent state of mind. His feet were badly frostbitten and he was in a desperately helpless condition. It was an embarrassing position for the erstwhile antagonist, but one which Mills met in an entirely impersonal manner. He worked over the exhausted man, saved his feet, and perhaps his self-respect; for as it proved, he had been influenced to take part in the schemes of neighborhood malice against his own judgment and better instincts.

Among the Colorado opponents of the park were men who sincerely felt a national park was a detriment to the development of the State. One of these was Senator E. M. Ammons, later Governor of Colorado, with whom Enos had many friendly debating encounters. At a meeting of the Denver Chamber of Commerce in 1910, Ammons voiced his opinion that the agricultural value of some of the proposed territory forbade its being used for scenic purposes. On the western slope, he argued, both the mining and farming interest were endangered, saying, "We want tillage of the soil more than we want tourists." He feared that mining and prospecting would be ended if the proposed bill went through, and that valuable water rights would pass under federal control, to which he was firmly opposed. It is probable that he was well acquainted with the habits of the Forestry Bureau.

Mills had visioned that parks should be handled in a different manner, apart from politics and commercialism. He was advocating the need for the creation of a department of government, which he called "A Department of Parks and Recreation." It was not enough to set aside these wonderlands for the public, but they must have proper administration, by those especially fitted for and interested in the work. As he put it:

"At the present time the Agricultural Department and the Interior Department are fighting for the control of national parks. As a park enthusiast for the past thirty years, I beg to express the opinion that neither of these departments should control parks. In every emergency these departments have united to betray parks. The national parks are worthy of, and need, a department of their own."

Congressman John S. Flower, in his address to the same meeting of the chamber joined Mills and proclaiming the tourist industry is infinitely more profitable than agriculture in the particular region at issue, citing Switzerland as an example of the paying asset that could be made of scenery.

After a long and heated session, the Chamber passed a resolution favoring the creation of the Estes National Park and Game Preserve, and urged that all members work for that end at the next session of Congress.

Similar meetings were held throughout the State, not once,

but time and again, until sufficient endorsements of a National Park for Colorado were secured. It devolved upon Mills to do most of the talking in behalf of the park, though many ardent supporters helped, calling meetings and getting the objectors to air the question in general debate. Gradually, most of the difficulties were ironed out.

With the national park idea taking hold, Mills suggested a larger plan, dumbfounded people by urging that eventually the area should include that stretch of parkland running along or near the crest of the Divide, and take in the major scenic attractions from Medicine Bow to Pikes Peak. These areas would be opened up by roads and trails for the greater enjoyment of the tourists. It was a magnificent conception, as the "Rocky Mountain News" commented in an editorial on Mills: "When completed it would be an asset of inestimable value. The tourist who failed to travel it north to south or south to north could not say that he had seen America."

But this extension of national park territory brought out strenuous opposition, not only from some of the people directly concerned, but from the Forestry Bureau who had only been lying low for a new point of attack on the bill.

It became of vital importance to define clearly the differences between a national forest and a national park, to establish in the mind of the public the special benefits of each, and the increasing necessity for separating the administration of the two as far as possible. Campaigning for a new department—new policies and adequate appropriations—for all national parks went on hand in hand with the efforts to put through the bill for the new one.

On this topic, Stuart Edward White wrote:

"If the public in general understood the difference between a national park and a national forest, there could be no doubt as to the opinion of any intelligent citizen. The distinction is so simple that it seems that it should be easy to get it within the comprehension of anybody. A national forest is a going business, carried on by the Government for the sale of timber and timber products, as far as it can be done without detriment to the property. A national park is an open-air Museum, set apart by Congress, either to preserve from commercial development beautiful scenery, trees, natural monuments, or some of the forests that are being cut commercially both in private and national forests. The idea is not commercial development along even conservative and constructive lines, but absolute preservation in a state of nature. Once this distinction is grasped, no one can doubt that these two institutions demand entirely different management. It would be as sensible to put men with the same training in charge of both national park and national forest, as it would be to place the same men with the same training in charge of a busy shoe factory and a museum of archaeology."

Many of Mills's recommendations and comments are set forth in "Your National Parks," under the title, "New Parks and Park Development." The broad scope of his work to have more people enjoy the recreational, educational, and inspirational benefits of the wilderness, became crystallized in the national park idea.

In 1912, Robert B. Marshall, chief geographer of the Department of the Interior, was sent out to Estes Park by President Taft to report on the area under consideration, Mills guaranteeing his expenses. His report silenced for all time the contention raised by the Forest Service and its allies, that the region was not worthy of recognition by the government as a national park. In this report the name was changed to "The Rocky Mountain National Park," the area was mapped and described by natural boundaries, rather than the former cut-and-dried land descriptions—eliminating most of the private property, and thereby silencing some local opposition. The proposed area included a twenty-five-mile stretch of the Continental Divide, lying about equally on eastern and western slopes, and from twelve to twenty miles in width. In only a few places did the proposed boundary, come below nine thousand feet, while more than fifty peaks over two miles high rose within it. The area included about three hundred and sixty square miles, while the center of the park was about fifty-five miles northwest of Denver, as the crow flies, and about sixty southwest of Cheyenne.

Following on the publication of Marshall's report, the papers took up the theme anew, wrote editorials about the Park and about the man who was promoting it. Another impetus was added in 1913 by Mills's revival of the "See America First" slogan, that dated back, probably, to Charles F. Lummis, the originator of the phrase in 1890. The "Chicago Inter-Ocean," in an editorial in March, asserted that the See-America-First movement appealed to the American people from every viewpoint: "The average American is a compound of sentiment and business sense. And Mr. Mills hits him both ways."

Mills's own interest was on the sentimental side, as the newspaper phrased it. He wanted the playgrounds for the people as reservoirs of health and beauty, places for recreation. People, he often stated, are made in their leisure hours. If some of that leisure could be spent in the lovely heart of Nature, they would benefit immeasurably. But he was astute enough to realize that in addressing civic clubs and business associations, he must also be able to prove that such playgrounds were to be counted on as good investments. It was not difficult to make men see that people spent money on vacations, and that vacations took too many out of the country. He began to preach "Make America ready to be seen."

But his lecture tours were not all grim attacks on the battlefront. Of one of them, J. Horace McFarland writes:

"At my request he came to a meeting of the American Civic Association in Washington, and told some stories one evening when President Taft was anticipated, but did not come when expected. Right in the midst of Mr. Mills's bear story, the President arrived and was seated. Very shortly thereafter his official aides tried to get him to go to some other engagement, but he refused, because he was so keenly enjoying Mr. Mills's stories, as Taft expressed himself to me very freely when he came to go. Afterwards, Mr. Mills came to me and said that he ought to have some notice if I was going to spring Presidents on him in that fashion. He needed no notice! I was with him on the firing line many other times and he could always make an audience realize the great spaces in the Rockies, the depth of the snow, the breadth of the view, and the immense advantages we could have in owning for the Government these unreplaceable natural features. His books are classics, and their general circulation and use, particularly by young people, will tend to build a better Americanism."

Mills was probably at his best when telling some of his incomparable bear stories. He was ever to defend them, to bespeak a kindly word for their native intelligence, courage and curiosity, and to urge the protection of bears in order that they might be more generally observed and studied in their native environment. Of the bears in Yellowstone, he says in "The Grizzly":

"The park had a numerous grizzly population when it was made a wildlife preservation. The people who, in increasing numbers, visited the park carried no firearms and they were not molested by the grizzlies. After some 20 years of this friendly association, numbers of grizzlies, dyspeptic and de-moralized from eating garbage, and annoyed by the teasing of thoughtless people, became cross and lately even dangerous. But these bears cannot be called ferocious. Eliminating garbage piles and cease harassing the bears, and they will again be friendly...Tell me what a bear is fed and how, and I will tell you what the bear is—his disposition and health."

When Mills affirmed that he had tramped the wilds many years without a gun and never been attacked by grizzlies or other wild animals, it seemed incomprehensible to persons who liked to picture the wilds as peopled do with dangerous and ferocious beasts. Sometimes, in explaining why he did not carry a gun, Mills would ask, "Well, you don't like to shoot your friends, do you?"

He especially enjoyed retelling the story of the young sheepherder whom Lowell Otis Reese met in one of the loneliest spots in the Trinidad Mountains in California.

"Aren't you afraid to be out here all alone?" Reese asked.

"Afraid?" The boy replied; "what's there to be afraid of? There ain't no humans here."

The Hetch-Hetchy fight was in full swing in California, and Mills frequently heard from Muir during 1913. One letter reads:

"I shall always feel good when I look your way: for you are making good on a noble career. I glory in your success as a writer and lecturer and in saving God's parks for the welfare of humanity. Good luck and long life to you. Ever faithfully your friend."

Again: " I'm glad you never weary in well doing. We have another big Hetch-Hetchy fight on our hands...The Sierra Club counts on your help."

And another: "I am glad to hear of your continued good health and good work in the cause of saving some of God's best mountain handiwork for the benefit of humanity and all our fellow mortals vertical or horizontal. Strange that the Government is so slow to learn the value of parks."

Muir died on Dec. 24, 1914, before the passing of the Rocky Mountain National Park Bill. In a talk immediately after Muir's death, at the Chicago Woman's Club, Mills said: "Muir felt keenly that the people of California were not in sympathy with him. The attitude weighed heavily upon his mind. He has often spoken of it to me. It was one of the tragedies of his life. John Muir, once he is understood, will be known as one of the great men of America. So much that he wanted to do for the Californians in enlarging their parks was turned down by them."

Mills broke his Eastern trips with returns to Colorado, to supervise winter work at the Inn. On these occasions Harry Walden would meet him in Estes Park with Mills's pony "Cricket" and he was soon reveling in the enjoyment of the mountain trails and the scenes that were so dear to him, and so full of refreshment. Mills loved horses and understood them, and for Cricket he had an unusual affection. Of her wisdom and alertness he has written in a number of sketches, one of which appeared in "The Rocky Mountain Wonderland"; others are still unpublished. Many of the Inn guests enjoyed in riding her, a privilege usually accorded to the more experienced, who would appreciate her intelligence. Even when nearing thirty years of age, Cricket retained her pep and alertness, and Mills's little daughter had the companionship of her last years.

During the fall of 1913, much snow fell around Estes Park and remained all winter. When Mills returned, the middle of December, it took him two days from Denver, by train, sled, horseback, and snowshoes, to reach his mountain cabin. A few days after arrival he had a call from a bighorn sheep. Putting on snowshoes he went out for a closer acquaintance and close-up pictures of this master of the crags. The caretaker was sent to the Inn for more films, and when he returned, the ram was contentedly eating grass in a windswept space where the snow was comparatively thin. This wildest of wild animals seemed to have little fear of the two men. But during the past seven years Mills had developed this confidence. The ram often came up to eat the salt which Mills kept for the pony, and by slow advances he had been able to make friends with it. So, it was not unexpected, by him, that on this winter day with deliberate, patient movements, he finally induced the ram to eat salt from his hand! The sheep had learned that he was in a wildlife reservation, as Mills tells in "Watched by Wild Animals."

The last three years of the park campaign were naturally the most strenuous. Man after man had to be won, and then held while others were being drawn into line. It was fine to get sincere and unexpected help, as often happened, from those who saw at once the importance of the issue and were glad to step up beside him. Estes Park was receiving much publicity, and the summer attendance increased from some 30,000 in 1912 to more than 55,000 in 1914.

The creation of the park seemed a certainty with each opening session of Congress. But the Colorado delegation, for some reason, were not giving it their entire and undivided support, although ostensibly endorsing the project. Bills for the Rocky Mountain National Park and the National Park Service were now before Congress. The bill for the park had been recast to meet all demands, assuring protection of private interests, water rights, mining claims, and roads already existing in the area. When Sen. Charles Thomas still did not fall in line, Mills wrote him that the mining district around the old town of Lulu, on the western slope, had been excluded from the area proposed. Senator Thomas immediately wired back that if there was no more mineral in the proposed Rocky mountain national Park than he had found at Lulu, he was for the bill. He proceeded to push it energetically and quickly got it through the Senate. Some months later, the Honorable E. T. Taylor put the bill through the House. Republican Leader Mann, of Illinois, who had been expected to oppose the measure, came out in favor of it. The Park became a reality in January, 1915.

Colorado papers published the news in immense headlines and everyone celebrated. An editorial in the "Denver Post" gave the credit where it belongs:

"It was Enos A. Mills who conceived the idea of conserving Nature's wonderful workmanship in the Long's Peak region, by placing it in the keeping of the United States Government, and, single-handed, he set out to accomplish this result. Single-handed, he brought it about, for all the forces that contributed to the victory were lined up through his efforts. Others have helped, to be sure, but it was Enos Mills's persistent labor that made them supporters of the movement.

"He fought against apathy at home and active opposition in Washington. The lack of interest that existed in Colorado he finally turned into enthusiasm. He had already aroused more public interest in the East then he found at home.

"For six years, every fall and winter when he might have put in his time on work with personal profit, he has traveled through the East, preaching Colorado scenery and the national park, paying his own expenses. He has lobbied at Washington with all the persistence and energy of the paid advocate of some special interest. He has written thousands and thousands of letters to men and organizations all over the country to enlist them in his cause. He has visited editors of great newspapers and magazines and won their support.

"Besides the time devoted to this campaign it has been expensive financially, for he has spent between $6000 and $7000 of his own money in furthering a movement that will be worth millions to Colorado.

"So let Colorado take off its hat to Enos Mills, who has nationalized the State's most beautiful park and capitalized Colorado's scenery, in which every citizen is a stockholder and dividend participant."

During these six years the national interest in scenery had broadened enormously. There was not a State in the Union now that was not aware of national parks, and there was hardly one that did not wish to secure such a park for itself. If not a national park, then a state park.

Mills kept on reminding Americans, especially Congressmen, that the only way to have this and other parks taken care of, as they should be, was to have them in charge of men trained for the work, men who really appreciated parks for their essential values. The history of park administration had been haphazard and without definite aim, and at the time the thirteen national parks and twenty-eight national monuments belonging to the nation were under the charge of a single clerk; also there had never been proper provision made for building and maintaining roads and trails so that people could thoroughly see the parks already existing.

In September, 1911, Secretary of the Interior Walter L. Fisher called the first National Park Conference in Yellowstone National Park. In 1914, Mark Daniels became the first superintendent by Secretary Franklin K. Lane's appointment. Robert B. Marshall, former chief geographer of the United States Geological Survey, became the superintendent of parks in 1915.

The National Park Service bill was introduced by Congressman Kent of California and finally passed in January, 1916. In March, 1917, Stephen T. Mather, former assistant to the Secretary of the Interior under Secretary Lane, became the director of the National Park Service.

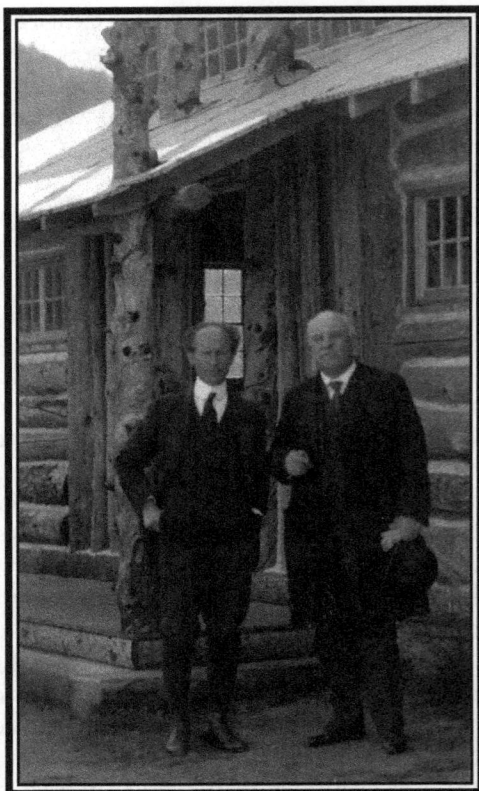

Enos with
Franklin K. Lane outside
Long's Peak Inn.

In January, 1917, a National Park Conference was held in the auditorium of the new National Museum in Washington, DC. The three-day session called together an impressive array of people: Franklin K. Lane, Secretary of the Interior; Stephen T. Mather, his Assistant; J.B. Harkin, Commissioner of the Dominion Parks of Canada; J. Horace McFarland; Henry S. Graves, Chief of the Forest Service; Marion Randall Parsons, of the Sierra Club of California; W. A. Welch, of the Palisades Interstate Park; Herbert Quick, Emerson Hough, and many more. Enos Mills presided at the special meeting to consider "The Recreational Use of the National Parks." In his special topic for discussion—"The National Parks for All the People"— he first expressed his opposition to the granting of mono-polistic concessions—an issue that was to call for the greatest effort of his life, and to array against him forces that were building up tremendous powers for political and commercial intrigue.

At the end of the Conference he gave an evening of bear stories.

Enos and Esther's daughter, Enda,
looks at anemonies with her teddy bear.

Home Ties

"Those who live pioneer lives are generally the most fortunate of people. To build a log cabin on the fresh wild mountainside and by its frontier fireplace explore the fairyland of enchanting thought, is indeed a blessing."
  Enos A. Mills

Amid all the excitement and celebration over the new national park, which had created news and noise for seven years, Mills went home early in the spring of 1916 to settle down to writing. Now, perhaps, he could complete the national park book, which was to contain the accumulated information and observations of twenty-five years of exploration and study. It was not to supplant Muir's "Our National Parks," that magnificent volume of descriptive literature that will live for all time; but rather to supplement it, to give more detailed and popular accounts of the varied attractions, in a form available for the tourist. The title of "Your National Parks" was chosen with the definite idea of instilling into the public consciousness a sense of responsibility for their future care and development.

The demands, however, for publicity material, photographs of the new Rocky Mountain National Park, and for articles on guiding and scenery and travel, constantly interrupted his plans. Finally, with the necessity of putting on his summer crew and supervising the hotel operations, the book had to be laid aside.

The Inn opened the first of May, somewhat ahead of the other hotels, and it often happened that people who along came even earlier were taken in, for Mills contended that all seasons with Nature were good, and "that time is best when you can stay the longest." He made it possible, so far as he could, for people to come at any time.

The summer was filled with plenty of activity, including a forest fire, ignited by a carelessly thrown match on the Fourth of July, that for a time threatened to take the entire valley. Mills's quick action and his knowledge of firefighting, directing effective volunteer work, prevented a widespread calamity.

In addition to his daily routine, there was never an hour in the day without its quota of callers; people came from near and far and brought their friends to meet the man, rather than the hotel proprietor; others to have him autograph his books or beautiful photographs; a few with no purpose except to satisfy their curiosity; and some who seriously discussed conservation or national park work, and hoped to enlist his aid in projects of their own.

Mills greeted his guests each morning with unchanging simplicity, and his "Glad you're living?" had the perennial freshness and spontaneity of the mountain flowers. To each of his guests he gave the maximum of attention, whether it was to the details of personal comfort or making suggestions for climbing the Peak. To see him in his role of host, one would scarcely believe that he had become a national figure, recognized and welcomed wherever he went.

The incentive to Western travel had received a sudden and tremendous boost with the closing of European gateways during the World War, and Colorado received its full share of visitors. How much of this sudden interest might be traced to Mills's lectures and articles on Colorado scenery is hard to say, but Arthur Chapman, who had been a newspaper man in the State for twenty years and in a position to know, wrote in "Country Life," 1920:

"Mills's writings have done more to establish Colorado as a public playground than all the tons of railroad resort literature ever published. If the State had capitalized Enos Mills it would have realized many hundred per cent on its investment. Yet there is not a note in his work that does not ring true. He has written spontaneously of the things which other men might have seen but could not."

In common with other hotels in the region, Mills started in early fall to enlarge his plant. Though the capacity season was very short, it was a great disappointment to turn people away in midsummer, and Mills's policy was to be ahead of the game, rather than let it overtake him. An electric light plant had been installed at the beginning of the summer, and additional modern cabins added in the last three years, but he must now increase the living and dining room capacity, and kitchen adjuncts, to fulfill the requirements.

It was fortunate that Mills had that happy faculty of being able to turn from one kind of work to another, finding a certain kind of rest—the only kind he wanted—in a change of activities. He was still running a capacity house in September, but the work must be started if he was to find time later to keep some lecture dates in the East. Then, with a crew busy on the proposed additions, he returned to his writing, his forthcoming "Your National Parks."

Esther Burnell was a guest at the Inn, and, like many another, reveling in the glorious mountain land that made city life look pale and colorless by comparison. It occurred to her that with a temporary job she might prolong her vacation. Mills was looking for someone to increase his clerical staff, and she gladly accepted. When not working on the book, Miss Burnell used every opportunity to get out into the surrounding country. She brought in comments on new beaver work and other observations that interested Mills. He delighted, too, in the fact that she sometimes followed the trails again at night, and even went off alone in a snowstorm. Before the Inn closed that fall, he offered her a position as secretary.

However, Miss Burnell had already decided to take up a homestead and spend the winter, if an available tract could be found. There were many others homesteading at the time, or proving up on claims filed some three, four, or five years earlier, both men and women, most of them living alone. It had been a lifelong dream of hers, and this seemed the time and the opportunity to realize it. When she was rebuked by women guests at the Inn for her long, lonely rambles, she explained that she was trying to locate a claim. They were doubly horrified; it seemed like throwing one's life away so completely to sever the strings of civilization. When she assured them that that was just what she wanted to do, they tried to impress her with the risks and dangers. Again she tried to calm their fears, declaring it was the safest place in the world to tramp and explore, in fact the best place to enjoy fully the outdoors, free from the limitations of fear and worry. As for Mills, he neither encouraged nor discouraged the plan.

Meantime, considerable snow had fallen and continued to fall. It was one of those exceptional years when winter comes in October and leaves no one in doubt as to its intention to stay. The building operations had been seriously handicapped; logs and building stone were buried beyond easy reach, and Mills had to devote much time to finding the necessary material. Also, he was unable to get his friend, Carl Pitz, to build the new fireplace, because of the many other demands on his time, and Mills designed one of his own and supervised the laying of the stonework. The whole was of mammoth proportions, occupying a full corner of the big room, with raised stone hearth, eighteen inches above the floor. Needless to say, work on the book had temporarily halted.

On the train to Denver, to keep a lecture date in St. Louis, Mills met Miss Burnell.

"Not leaving the country, I hope!" he exclaimed.

"No, just coming in, on my way to file a homestead."

He had thought perhaps she would abandon the plan with the unpropitious weather, and the difficulties of getting workmen at that time of the year to put up a cabin. But he discussed none of this as he took a seat beside her. He talked about the importance of having a hobby, something to interest one outside of his daily thought and activity. Some phase of nature, he told her, was the best hobby people could have, because it took them into healthful and beautiful scenes while furnishing abundant material for reflection. "Getting people interested in Nature, helping to give them the resource of their own out-of-doors, has been my lifework. That is why I am talking nature guiding intensively. We need more guides. Better consider it."

After his lecture appointment, Mills returned to finish his book, and then went East for several months. There were important interviews on national park questions, and numerous speaking engagements, and a National Park Conference in Washington. Incidentally, he took issue with the then Superintendent of the Rocky Mountain National Park over the question of women guiding, the latter contending that they were unsuited to the profession. But Mills won his point, and stressed the importance of featuring natural history in a popular manner, as the coming need in national park use and development.

The climax of his discussion was his attack on the policy of granting monopolistic concessions in the people's playgrounds. It came as a bombshell; no one was prepared for it. As usual, Mills was a step ahead. He could see that the trend of the Director was toward concessions. He protested bitterly against the great injustice that monopolies would inflict on the newly created Rocky Mountain National Park, where private enterprise had been developing the region for fifty years, and where the public had become accustomed to expect and enjoy the advantages of competitive service and charges. It was only the wild life, the forests, and natural beauty that needed protection; the travelers were being adequately provided for. Roads and trails needed improvement and extension, the park needed appropriations—but not exploitation.

It was not a promising outlook. He hoped against hope that his arguments had been convincing. But he was prepared for another fight if need be, to protect the region, and the travelers to it, in harmony with the spirit and wording of the bill, which had been studiously prepared to exclude monopolistic concessions.

When he returned to Long's Peak in the spring of 1917, he started his campaign against concessions. He wrote to all the supporters of the national park cause, to impress upon the unsuspecting the need of keeping a watchful eye on Washington. The work of the seven years in having the Park set aside for the nation would not be lost if everyone would stay on the job. But it could not be left to politicians and the ever-aggressive commercial interests. He wrote an article for the "Saturday Evening Post," called, "Where Rolls the Hudson," demonstrating how a park could, and should, be run—without profiteering concessions. He described the usefulness of the Palisades Interstate Park of New York and New Jersey, under the direction of W. A. Welch and Commissioner George W. Perkins and the ideal manner in which it was managed.

He was no less active in his nature writing, for every day that he could catch between seasons meant more bear stories, more trailing of otter or antelope or sheep, or being trailed, and watched, by mountain lions. He had an inexhaustible fund of experiences from which to draw, and he wanted the reading public to share in them, perhaps be inspired to follow the trails in quest of similar adventure. That so many have done so is due in no small degree to his constant preaching, "The wilderness is friendly, wild animals not ferocious, all weather is good, and altitude, the bugbear of many, is beneficial."

One day when he was riding cross-country on Cricket, he took occasion to stop and see how Miss Burnell the homesteader was faring. She was busy planting potatoes and enjoying it, but not too busy to show Mills over her homestead. They even climbed to the top of Castle Mountain to get the view of Long's Peak, some twelve miles away. The view was not new to Mills, even from this point, for he had been over the region many times in his early rambles around and all over the mountains. But the enthusiasm of the homesteader was refreshing. As she spoke of her enjoyment of the winter trails, the slow coming of spring with its first anemones and returning birds, of the sheep and deer that had been around her cabin all winter, he was reminded of his boyhood cabin and the days of sheer delight that he had spent there.

"Yes," he told her, quoting his favorite Stevenson, "to miss the joy is to miss all." He forgot monopolies for the time being, and explored mountaintops with all the exuberance of a boy again.

Mills discussed some of the stories he was writing, for he always liked to get the reactions of an audience before putting them into print. He found a sympathetic listener, and one who had many questions to ask, which encouraged him to put more of his personal experiences into them. Esther admitted, when pressed, that she had been trying her hand at some stories. Mills offered to read them. In return Esther offered to do such typewriting as she could find time for if he would send over the copy. And thereupon developed an exchange of manuscripts, which to the neighbors who carried the mail looked like a voluminous correspondence.

"I always enjoy anyone who has resources enough to live alone," Mills said, in leaving, "who has the independence to go

Enos with Esther Burnell examining a stump.

off the beaten track." But, not too much off the beaten track, he thought to himself, as he started Cricket on the twelve miles homeward. There would not be much further opportunity for calling; time was at a premium, and he did not drive a car.

He was asked to talk before the Estes Park Woman's Club that May and suggested to his hostess that she invite Esther Burnell. Mills took for his subject "A Goldfinch Romance"—an incident of bird study in his early boyhood which he had never before told. He hoped it might interest at least one of the women present; at any rate, he directed his attention that way during the telling, hoping to get her response to the story. The concentration was not lost on his audience; neither was his dash across the room, at the end of it, to claim as seat beside her on the couch.

The meeting was held in the lounge of the Stanley Manor, and it was a rather obvious dash across the big room, especially when a number of other ladies nearer were waiting to express their comments. One of them followed Mills and took a seat beside him on the couch. Mills unconsciously crowded Esther on the other side. There was a hearty laugh over this, in which Mills joined, and everyone felt relieved. But numbers of the audience wanted to congratulate the speaker, which kept him bobbing up and down in lively fashion and greatly interrupting the visit which he had been looking forward to having with the homesteader.

However, Miss Burnell did find an opportunity to tell him that she was delighted with his story, and hoped he would put it into print. They continued to talk it over for some time, and finally realized that the room was empty but for themselves. The audience had politely withdrawn and allowed them to have their visit out. But the women tingled with the atmosphere of romance that had permeated the afternoon, and rumors of the engagement of the couple were whispered about.

"A Goldfinch Romance" was one of the next stories written, to be published in "The American Boy Magazine" and later in "Bird Memories of the Rockies." It reveals not only an insight into the tender associations of bird life, but the underlying sweetness of Mills's nature and his discriminating appreciating of the finer qualities of character, whether in bird or human.

"Your National Parks" was out in late spring, and Mills

Enos with Esther outside Long's Peak Inn.

took occasion to go over to "Keewaydin" as the homestead was called, and present Esther Burnell with a copy. But, more important, he had come to say:

"If you can get away for the summer, I will give you some real live bear material to keep you busy and excited. The grizzly is to feature the next book."

As usual, as soon as one book was out, and often before, he was planning for the next one.

"I read your 'Guides Wanted' in the 'Post,'" Esther answered. "I was thinking of applying."

"It looks as though the profession would be over-crowded," Mills replied, after a little thought. "I have already received letters from hundreds of applicants since I wrote my 'Guiding in National Parks' for 'Country Life' a year ago. But the bears are in danger of extermination. They need pro-tection," he added, turning toward her with his contagious smile.

The afternoon wore on, with talk of books and writing. Mills quoted Stevenson again: "But we are all travelers in the wilderness of this world, all, too, travelers with a donkey; and the best that we find in our travels is an honest friend. He is a fortunate voyager who finds many. We travel, indeed, to find them. They are the end and reward of life."

July found Esther at the Inn, where her sister Elizabeth

joined her. Together they explored the trails in their spare time from Inn duties, sleeping out at night and thrilling with all the delights of new discoveries. Elizabeth started a flower exhibit, arranging individual flowers in slim vases marked with their popular names, to help guests in their flower studies. It took much time, and soon absorbed most of the day, for people from the surrounding region began bringing in specimens to be identified. Mills always cautioned her against giving too much time to people who were capable of doing their own research work. The important thing, he said, was to incite interest in those who did not know how to begin, especially to deal in generalizations in flower stories.

Elizabeth brought with her to the Rockies a considerable range of experience in conducting outdoor activities. She was unusually qualified for guiding, having energy and enthusiasm, a ready interest in and sympathy for the work, and she soon became the most popular and versatile guide the region had seen. She was just the leader Mills wanted for the Trail School activities. She could take parties up Long's Peak, four or five times a week if it so happened, plan a week's camping expedition with tenderfeet in Wild Basin, induce timid guests to sleep out on top of Twin Sisters to see the sunrise, explore beaver colonies with men, women and children, take a nature study group around the yard to find nesting birds, and give popular talks on natural history and outdoor subjects before the evening audiences. She continued in the nature guiding at the Inn for twelve summers, meantime giving up her teaching of higher mathematics, in which she had received her M. A. at the University of Michigan, to become supervisor of nature study in the Los Angeles City Schools.

It was one of the busiest summers Mills had ever had. Though it had doubled its capacity in the last five years the Inn was overflowing. In fact, the entire region was visited by such crowds as had never been imagined possible. The general verdict seemed to be that the Rocky Mountain National Park was a success. Everyone who came was enthusiastic, and many built beautiful summer homes with the intention of becoming regular visitors.

The Inn always harbored an interesting group. There were royal evenings, with the guests seated in a large semicircle in front of the great fireplace, mostly fresh from a long day in the open, dressed in khaki, or in boots and riding clothes—for informality was a feature of the place. Mills might talk of bears, of mirages, of lightning and thunder, snow slides, avalanches, trees or birds. Someone else would then take a turn; it might be about poetry, science, travel, adventure, botany, the stage, or all of these. They did not need, and did not want, bridge and dancing to entertain them.

Even the busiest of summers must come to an end. After rounding out a few weeks of writing, Mills went East in an effort to learn more of the concession policies of the National Park Service. From various sources he learned that "concessions were necessary in national parks"; "the public require regulations to insure safety and accommodations"; or he was asked, "What's your objection to a transportation concession?" Mills was ready with facts to prove that the use and development of parks had been seriously handicapped by the elimination of competitive transportation facilities, and by the granting of exclusive franchises for business necessities. Overtures were made to Mills to cease his opposition, with promises of sufficient weight to tempt the average person. But not Mills. His convictions were based on principle, the same principle for which he had already made many sacrifices. He was committed to his self-imposed task of keeping the park open to the public.

It was fortunate for Mills that his faculty of being able to turn from one interest to another prevented his becoming entirely caught in the entanglements of political maneuvering. Having done all he could for the movement, he would bide his time, go home, take up other work.

When he returned to the mountains, he always visited the homestead, where Esther and Elizabeth had spent the winter. He enjoyed hearing of their successful preparation for guiding, of the tramping they had done about the mountains. There was no talk of discouraging factors in the park management, or of the problems that war measures had brought in limiting food stuffs, and experimenting with substitutes. With all of his other projects, he was always lending a helping hand to those who were just getting started; he liked to see people succeed, whether in mountain climbing, building a hotel, launching conservation work, or learning to write. Ambitious writers, especially, were sure of encouragement. He even encouraged the children at the Inn to write down comments on their outings, and to talk to him about their observations. His questions often incited them to go and look again.

One of the steps taken that summer by the Forest Service to gain back its lost territory was to have the national parks opened to grazing, as "an emergency measure". Yet millions of acres of undeveloped land throughout the West, more suited to the purpose, were available. Another serious situation developed in the attempt to prevent the opening of the hotel as a "nonessential" and as interfering with the conservation of food products. Mills had gained enemies in his determined convictions who were doing their best to ruin him; but he also had friends, and occasionally he used them.

But his guests never knew of these side issues. For them life went serenely on; talking with Mills, wandering over the trails, enjoying the pleasant society of congenial folk. And so Mills wanted it, each day full to the brim with new experiences for these city-bound people, who had such brief opportunity to enjoy the mountains. His enthusiasm was contagious, and his personality left a deep impression on all who met him. His friendship was claimed by many who had only the slightest acquaintance with him, but they had felt his sincere and sympathetic interest in what they were trying to do in the world. Mills enjoyed meeting anyone who was working with a definite aim, and unconsciously drew to him and about him a surprising number of prominent and successful people in all professions—writers, lawyers, artists, actors, university professors, editors, and financiers. With it all, the school teacher or clerk on a limited stipend, received as much of Mills's time and attention as those of national fame. The hospitality all alike received at the Inn created a kind of democracy; people made friends without being introduced—without having to know who or what the other fellow was. They were brought together by their common interest in the outdoors, in simple, wholesome activities. As Mills said on many occasions, "The trail promotes acquaintance; it demands our best."

During this busy spring and summer, Mills found time withal to pursue his courtship of Esther Burnell, under difficulties, to be sure, tied to the Inn as he was six months of the year, and she occupied with her homesteading. But the wedding day was finally set for August 12, 1918. The strictest secrecy had prevailed. The news leaked out as soon as the licence was issued, and was rapidly circulated. The simplest of ceremonies took place in Mills's little homestead cabin under the eyes of Elizabeth and a few associates. To be sure, there were a number of disappointed guests, but in his personal affairs Mills was peculiarly reticent. This was one instance in which public interest was not needed. But it came, nevertheless. Letters and telegrams of congratulations poured in by the hundreds. In Mills's estimation, the words which best fitted the occasion were received in a telegram, "Though the Mills of the Gods grind slowly, they grind exceedingly fine."

Work went on as before—only harder and more of it. There were the usual demands at the Inn, and some unusual ones. Mills knew so well the intricacies of the organization that he was not even surprised when the unexpected happened. He kept his finger on each detail, was the first to know of a broken main, the failure of the freight truck to arrive, or the need for a rescue party for someone lost or injured. And he was always prepared for the solution of whatever problem arose.

The happiness of each guest was still as important to him as in the first days of his hotel enterprise. He had a marvelous faculty of never seeming to be hurried, of giving the impression that his entire time was at the disposal of his guests. It was as restful to meet and talk with him as to pause on one of his trails under the whisper of the pines. On the other hand, there was no lost motion about him, and every minute counted.

When the Inn closed in late October, Mr. and Mrs. Mills settled down in their cabin, simply equipped for housekeeping, with the prospect of much writing, some tramping, and a little quiet time to themselves, all of which had been excluded by the necessities of the hotel life.

"The Grizzly, Our Greatest Wild Animal," was completed for spring publication, 1919, by Houghton Mifflin Company. Its reception was in every way as cordial as Mills's own acquaintance with the animal himself had been. It was a surprise and a delight to readers to learn, for the first time, that bears play, that they travel, that they have curiosity—and many other appealing characteristics. Most unbelievable of all, they were told that grizzlies are not ferocious and never attack man unless antagonized or demoralized by garbage meals. Mills had made extensive, close up studies of grizzlies, through a long period of years, and he had done his trailing without a gun! The book serves a threefold purpose—to entertain, to educate, and to help protect the species.

Enos with his mother, Ann,
during her visit to Long's Peak Inn.

During the first four months of the year 1919, ten lengthy stories were written on animals, adventure, geology, and educational uses of Nature, to be published in the "Saturday Evening Post" within the year. Mills was supremely happy, doing the thing he enjoyed most. It was the first winter in many years that he had not made at least one Eastern lecture tour, far harder to him than these months of writing.

On April 27 he sent forth the biggest piece of news, in his estimation, that had ever gone forth from that mountain valley: "We have a red-headed girl baby at our house!" As time passed Enda developed the greatest attachment for her father, and seemed to consider his time and attention her natural birthright, while it is difficult to imagine a more elated or devoted parent. There was scarcely an hour during that summer that he did not make opportunity in his hotel routine to run into his cabin with a smile and a "Hello" to Enda.

Meanwhile, "The Adventures of a Nature Guide" had been completed, to be published in 1920, followed by "Waiting in the Wilderness" in 1921, "Watched by Wild Animals" in 1922, and "Wild Animal Homesteads" in 1923.

Enda was always content if she could be in the room while her father was dictating, amusing herself with books, pictures, or her "Teddy-Bear." Then, when her mother went to the typewriter, what great times she and her father had!

The Last Stand

"Over his clouds the lark still sang,
And when the night was gone,
Thrilling the dark of the outer gloom,
His nightingale sang on."
　　　　Lines written to Stevenson

In 1919, the Department of the Interior, through Stephen T. Mather, Director of the National Park Service, granted an exclusive transportation concession to the Rocky Mountain Parks Transportation Company of Estes Park, in reality the White Automobile Company for the hauling of passengers and freight through the Rocky Mountain National Park. This was secretly given, and was not made public until the operation of the summer's business opened, too late to meet the issue. No bids had been asked in granting the concession. Under the guise of getting local people to approve the transportation facilities already operating in Estes Park, endorsements of the Rocky Mountain Parks Transportation Company were secured to satisfy official requirements; but at the time these endorsements were given by the residents, it was without the knowledge that other transportation facilities would be abolished in favor of one of the company, and that independent carriers would be eliminated. However, in order to safeguard their own business, these signers qualified their endorsement with the suggestion that "if monopolies in various lines of service were to be granted, they be considered for such concessions." In other words, instead of taking a definite stand against favoritism in the administration of the park, they were hand in glove with the National Park Service policies.

It must be remembered that Estes Park, the center of the business activities of the travelers to the region, was some eight miles from the boundaries of the National Park. As yet no restrictions had been placed upon the use of the park, the appropriations for the local administrative force not being sufficient to provide much interference. In was therefore impossible for the people to realize what authority would be enforced, not only upon visitors, whose interests should have been paramount, but also upon the continued development of their own lines of business, once a government-granted and government-protected monopoly took control. They were to learn that Washington is a long way off and officials there far too busy or indifferent to explain the new regime to travelers or straighten out difficulties which local conditions produce.

For fifty years the scattered population of Estes Park had jogged along in a rut of least resistance, accepting what came of success or popularity, of recent years in such abundance, with the minimum of personal effort. They had not made the attractions and they had developed little appreciation of their value. Civic or community pride was almost wanting, and progressive cooperation next to impossible. Any suggestions for improvement in the town or expansion of the outlying trails was considered a reflection on the "good old days". With it all, the town had progressed of its own momentum; but the general attitude of the majority remained the same.

It was difficult to explain the intricate workings and inter-locking alliances of a monopoly to the natives of Estes Park, at the time when Mills endeavored to forewarn them; but many have since learned from sad experience. In order to appreciate the result of giving special privileges in National Parks and the background of Mills's convictions, it might be well to turn back a few years to see what a similar monopoly produced in Yellowstone National Park.

Yellowstone, the oldest of national parks, had long been in the hands of a monopoly, and the people of Cody, Wyoming, backed by the State itself, had, during Taft's administration, sent a strong protest to Secretary of the Interior Fisher. By far the most beautiful entrance to the park is from Cody up the marvelous Shoshone Canyon. The State of Wyoming had built an excellent automobile road up the canyon, with the hope of winning tourists to enter by this gateway, known as the Sylvan Pass Entrance, but it was found that the Yellowstone Park Hotel Company, the Wylie Camp and the Yellowstone Park Transportation Company held control over the transportation and tourist business of the Park. The complaint cited the fact that the people of Cody had been refused permission by the Secretary to establish camps in the Park in order to accommodate tourists who came through that way. They were told to make arrangements with the monopoly. But the monopoly refused them the rates they asked, with the result that they were virtually excluded from Yellowstone. "This," said the complaint, "is due entirely to the fact that the monopoly now controlling this business is controlled in turn by men who have large political power in Washington and who are naturally opposed to the Cody route, as an entrance into the Park, because it would mean cutting down of business by the way of a hitherto popular entrance at Gardiner, Montana."

In plain words, Yellowstone Park was being run, not for the convenience and best interests of the people for whom it had been created, but for the profit of the monopoly.

The same conditions followed in the Rocky Mountain National Park. While the means which were used to support and defend the transportation monopoly exceeded all bounds. By main force of armed rangers, by threat and intimidation, the local people were hammered into nonresistance.

The peculiar character of the region surrounding the park made this system of road control particularly unjust. The business development was entirely outside the boundaries of the park. Tourists, whether in hotels or in their own private summer residences, of which there was now many, could not enjoy the attractions of the park without hiring a private car of the transportation monopoly, at exorbitant charges; while the regular bus service which they ran for their own convenience did not reach all sections of the region.

The numerous independent taxi drivers, who had formerly handled this irregular sightseeing business, were not allowed to operate across the boundaries of the park without permits from the Superintendent of the park; and these, of course, could not be secured, because he was under orders to protect the monopoly—to exclude competition with the franchised company.

Innumerable attempts were made by hotel cars and independent for-hire cars to exercise their legal rights to use the roads, but there met with the blockade of armed rangers paid by the taxpayers of the nation to protect the park rather than assist a privileged transportation company. There were many instances, of physical violence in these encounters when the resisting citizens were placed under arrest by the rangers, without warrants being issued. There was no opportunity for redress in the local courts. The ranger's word was law.

One of the drivers of a Long's Peak Inn car, because he attempted to take passengers into the park, was ejected by a ranger with the command, "not to enter the Park again for business, pleasure, or any purpose whatsoever."

Mills insisted that, in being deprived of his right to use the roads, he was denied the "full use and enjoyment of his land" contrary to the terms of the National Park Act. A suit was filed seeking an injunction restraining the Superintendent of the park from interfering with his right. While this was pending, a local driver, who had been ejected from the park of the Superintendent, brought suit against the Superintendent.

It was obvious that the rules and regulations promulgated by the Department of the Interior were not designed to give the public the freest use and enjoyment of the park, and Mills further contended that these regulations were not laws, subject to review by the local courts, but arbitrary provisions with no beneficial intention except to protect the monopoly.

Much of the coming fall and winter were taken up with getting the situation before those who had authority to correct the injustices. But when the national park policies were upheld, Mills proceeded to make these policies the subject of fiery and eloquent printed statements and letters circulated broadcast. In these he set forth the arguments in a clear and definite manner, and demanded that "permission be granted any reliable transportation company or individual—reliable by being a property owner or by giving bonds—to haul passengers through the national parks by complying with the traffic regulations of the parks."

The roads over which this authority was being enforced were state, county, and private roads, radiating from the center of Estes Park—roads excluded by the Act of Congress creating the Rocky Mountain National Park from jurisdiction of the Federal Government. The injustice to travelers was intensified by the arrogance and indifference of park officials. They did not want to recognize, and yet could not ignore entirely, the fact that many of these roads had been built by pioneers to open up remote regions where their private holdings were located. People were not allowed to enter the Park in any hired car not belonging to the enfranchised company even to reach their own property! A limited amount of private land had been included within the park boundaries, owing to the irregular topography of the mountain region, and owing also to the fact that roads had already made these regions accessible. But these private roads, though excluded from the government jurisdiction over the rest of the park, were watched by armed rangers.

Mills contended that the monopoly had been illegally granted and was being illegally operated. When the Superintendent telephoned him that the road from Estes Park to Long's Peak would be under the jurisdiction of a ranger at the point where the Park boundary crossed it, Mills announced that he himself would also be there to see that his guests were allowed unrestricted entrance and egress. Through such defiance he prevented any interference on the road which connected the Long's Peak district with the outside world—a road built year by year, during the past forty-five years, by the taxpayers of the county, and on which not a cent of national park appropriations had been spent.

But other hotel owners were not so firm, while the independent drivers, both local and from the adjacent towns of Loveland, Longmont, Boulder, and Denver, who had been showing tourists through the park region for many years, soon gave up the battle. This was just what the transportation monopoly wanted—not only the business through the park, but along the roads from Denver to the park. The park entrances were some thirty miles from the railroads, and hence the transportation question was the one vital factor in the enjoyment of the park.

Mills was not allowed to drive his guests for paid trips into other section of the park, because this was interfering with the business of the exclusive concessionaire. Yet he was too far from the transportation office to allow his guests to connect with the scheduled trips. Therefore a special car would have to be sent from Estes Park to Long's Peak to pick up these guests, take them on the desired trip, then return the guests to Long's Peak, with an empty trip back to Estes Park—one complete round trip at a cost of ten dollars which was entirely lost so far as the guest was concerned. Mills had from the beginning of his hotel enterprise made trips to Estes Park to get his guests; had, in fact, provided all of the transportation facilities for his guests, often making as many as three round trips a day with a Stanley Steamer to meet the Denver buses in Estes Park, these buses never having maintained service farther than Estes Park. It was the convenience of his guests that moved him— not the profit from the transportation business. But a transportation monopoly has no consideration other that profit; minimum service, maximum charges.

The situation which existed at Long's Peak was not unlike

that existing in other outlying sections of the Park. The trend of tourist travel was directed, most naturally, to the hotels most conveniently reached by the transportation schedule. Moreover, instead of lowering the charges—the argument on which the monopoly was granted—these charges were raised over preceding years, no adequate service rendered, and the whole scheme developed with the object of forcing travelers to go in crowded buses over the main routes, rather than allowing them to go where they wanted, and when they wanted, as had been their privilege under the former regime of numerous independent operators.

People began to go elsewhere for their vacations. One unpleasant experience with park rangers, or the inconvenience of changing to a monopoly car at the Park entrance, proving too annoying even for the privilege of enjoying the beauties awaiting them, of which they had heard so long and traveled hundreds of miles to see.

The Superintendent was harassed with complaints. The objectors were advised to take their troubles to Washington. Washington naturally upheld the monopoly. Tourists are generally too weary, or too disinterested, to resort to controversy. That a good many grievances did reach Washington, however, is a matter of fact. The Director of the National Park Service promised that there would be some changes for the better before another summer. The change? A new superintendent! The monopoly stayed.

That local people did finally become aroused is worthy of comment. They were intimidated, discriminated against, and told that they would be put out of business if they did not keep quiet—and some received all the punishment threatened. Others, when urged to act, responded with the bitterest of retorts: "We can't, we belong to the ―― outfit." The local company had shrewdly inveigled many into buying stock in this great money-making scheme, and so permanently silenced any criticisms of poor service or overcharges to tourists.

Soon it was circulated that "Mills was the only one opposed to the monopoly." Some tried to show that he wanted the transportation monopoly himself, and hence was fighting it. If Mills had been looking for a moneymaking proposition, he would not have chosen that one. It was at the antipodes of all to which he had devoted his life. If he had been looking for personal gain, he might better have saved his energy to devote

Enos while on tour in Montclair, New Jersey, January 2, 1922.

to his own business, instead of spending it so generously for the development of the region. To work for the common good without ulterior motive is a quality so rare that it is usually misjudged.

These attacks did not silence Mills. He paid no attention to them. He was far too busy with the real issue to be diverted by personalities, as the opposition hoped he would be.

Even if the region had not already been adequately supplied with transportation facilities, the monopoly would have been a mistake in Mills's estimation. The numerous travelers to national parks—whose dominating charm and immense value was the freedom, the individuality of Nature, the escape from iron-bound schedules—were being deprived of the chief requisites of a vacation. But the injustices of a monopolistic concession in the Rocky Mountain National Park, contrary to the spirit and the letter of its creation, were intolerable. This was his stand and he went to its defense, its exposition, with the same wholehearted determination that had governed his entire life.

Efforts to silence Mills by promises of benefits or threats of discrimination were useless. One might as well have tried to stop an avalanche in its course down a mountain. He was not fighting the personnel of the Park Service, or of the transportation company, or of any allied interest. He was fighting the system, a system which interfered with personal liberty and public rights.

The contest between bureaucracy and public rights was to be the story of the last five years of Enos Mills's life. Winter saw him on the trail—not of the snowy peaks he loved, but of the politician, the newspapers, the editors, the clubs and associations that might help the cause. It is tragic to watch the heroic struggle of this one man for his ideal, but it is also inspiring.

He could so easily just have done nothing. He would have got much by keeping still, and he would have been free to live his own life in the place and with the people he cared for. But he could not do it. The years might have stretched long and full and comfortable for him, filled with the work he preferred, in a growing prosperity and richness of life. But to this lover of individual independence the leveling down by autocratic control of public privilege was a growing menace to national life and liberty. He had work to do that interested him profoundly, and the wilderness where he was at home and happiest lay waiting at his door. But he turned from all this to fight against what proved impossible odds. He chose what was to him the right and only road. He reached the end of that road with his integrity and his honor unblemished and was able to say, "I have had a great life." There were no regrets.

Mills was not, as reported, the only one opposed to the government-granted monopolies in national parks. A letter from a California Congressmen, March 16, 1920, reads:

"Practically the entire California delegation are entirely out of line with the policy of the director of national parks, Mr. Mather, who is, by the way, a Californian. This gentleman is putting over a number of exclusive and monopolistic contracts in connection with the transportation and other concessions in our national parks, and we, as Californians, are strenuously objecting to the contract entered into with the outfit known as the Yosemite National Park Company, and intend at an early date to have a thorough airing of this whole matter before a Congressional Committee."

Mr. Henry B. Joy, of Detroit, in the "Boulder Camera," August, 1920, states:

"It was never intended by Congress that monopolistic

control of park facilities should be promoted as the result of the National Park Acts of Congress. It was never intended, for example, that in the Rocky Mountain National Park, one of the chief functions of governmental influence should be to use a large part of the Rocky Mountain National Park appropriation for the purpose of employing a Superintendent and staff of employees, one of whose important functions is to exert a repressive, restrictive, coercive influence in order that an exclusive concessionaire of the transportation monopoly granted in that part by the Secretary of the Interior should enjoy his rights to the detriment of the park development or to the detriment of any individual, properly and legitimately and warrantably, carrying on business in proper and legal matter within the boundaries of such a national park."

To a disinterested reader, the question of who conducts travelers through a national park might seem of slight significance. As Mr. Mills brought out in one of his printed circulars that went broadcast over the land, "Controlling of traffic through a national park gives control of traffic from the railroads to the park and also control of the merchants who sell supplies both within the park and the large outlying region which is inseparable in business from the park. Concessions feed a horde of politicians. It is axiomatic that monopolistic transportation has dictatorship over the industries, that is to say, over the people, within the territory controlled."

That the local people were almost completely dominated by the dictates of this concessionaire is shown in an article published in the "Denver Post," October, 1921, entitled "Estes Businessmen Condemn Fight Waged on Automobile Transportation Plan in Park."

There was one who was not influenced by the mob psychology, who had the vision to see the far-reaching influence of such propaganda as the above article had presented. Mr. F. O. Stanley replies to the "Denver Post" article, in the same paper, December, 1921:

"An article which appeared in a recent issue is so misleading and likely to cause so much harm, not only to Estes Park, but indirectly to the entire state of Colorado, that I, for one, cannot let it go unnoticed.

"In order that the reader may know what has been done, I will give a brief history of the Rocky Mountain National Park, as it was created and has been managed up to the present time.

"The first bill creating this part passed both branches of Congress and was signed by the President in January, 1915. The park as thus established was confined, largely, to the mountain district which was publicly owned and it included some private property, the practically none of the important roads in so-called Estes Park.

"Later it was thought best buy some to extend the park by including Deer Mountain, Twin Sisters, Gem Lake, and Miller Fork, all of which were publicly owned. In including these four points in the national park, it was not the intention of those proposing it to take in any more private property, but simply these isolated areas. But, when the line was run, it was so run as to include several thousand acres of private property, and some of the most important roads in Estes Park. And all this without the consent, and quite generally without the knowledge, of the landowners, and also without any compensation of any kind whatever. This addition was made in 1917, and at the time no one offered any objections.

"But in the year 1919, a most unusual thing happened. Without any notice of any kind, without any public hearing or competitive bids, an exclusive franchise for twenty years was given to one party, namely, the Rocky Mountain Transportation Company, to carry passengers back and forth into the national park. And at the time this franchise was given the Government had not spent one penny in building or repairing any road in the national park. And all the roads had been built by the counties or the State from funds raised by public taxation and private subscription.

"Could anything be more autocratic, unreasonable, or unjust? Take my own case as an example. In my 19 years in Estes Park, I have paid in taxes approximately $40,000, and in addition I have contributed, toward building roads in the park and the approaches to the park, over $15,000—and yet I am denied the full use of the roads; and what is true in my case is true, in different degrees, in the case of every taxpayer in the State.

"Of all the social problems man has had to consider, none has been more thoroughly solved than the road problem. Public roads are public property and can be used alike by all.

"The head of the richest corporation has no privilege on a public highway that is not shared by the humblest individual.

Whatever restriction is placed on the liberty of one in the use of the roads is placed on the liberty of all. If the poor man has to pay a tax on his low-priced automobile, the rich man has to pay a like tax, and in proportion to the value of his machine.

"So jealous are the people of their right to travel over the surface of the earth, if a private way is used by the public for a certain time without objection on the part of the owner, it then becomes a public highway, and the owner loses his control of it. I cite these well known facts merely to show how completely is the granting of a special franchise to one party to carry passengers into the national park contrary to established law and custom.

"I have mentioned above that when the addition to the park was made in 1917, taking in much private property, no one objected. And why should they? The original bill creating the national park seemed to afford ample protection to individual rights. A part of section 2 of that bill reads as follows: 'That nothing herein contained shall affect any valid existing claim, location, or entry, under the land laws of the United States, whether for homestead, mineral, right-of-way, or any other purpose whatsoever, or shall affect the rights of any such claimant, locator, or entryman, to the full use and enjoyment of his land.'

"Also, section 3 of the same bill reads, 'That no lands located within the park boundaries now held in private, municipal, or state ownership, shall be affected by or be subject to the provisions of this Act.'

"So it seemed to the owners of land in the national park that the bill itself protected them in the use of their land and in the use of the roads, hence no objections were raised. In fact, the entire tenor of the bill seemed to aim at making the park free to all. This is well expressed in section 4, a part of which reads: 'Said regulations being primarily aimed at the freest use of the park for recreation by the public.'

"Yet, in spite of the fact that the common law and custom in the use of the roads would prevent it, and the fact that the bill creating the park plainly would prohibit it, the park management makes the transportation of passengers in the park an absolute monopoly.

"Now, if there is any one thing that the people hate more than any other, it is a monopoly. Yet, some monopolies are absolutely necessary. Street cars, for instance. Here competition is necessarily eliminated. Either the cars must be owned and run by the city or by some private corporation under city control. But even here the public surrenders nothing, as all other vehicles have the full use of the roads.

"Also, some monopolies may be classed as legitimate monopolies. They start from small beginnings, and, by serving the public well, grow and develop in spite of the freest competition, until they become so large and efficient that they practically control some particular industry. But they are not harmful, for their very existence depends upon serving the public well and at low costs.

"Now, the monopoly we are questioning, namely, the transportation of passengers into the Rocky Mountain National Park, belongs to neither of these two classes, but is an officially created monopoly, contrary to the laws of our public highways, and openly in violation of the Act of Congress creating the national park, and from the nature of the circumstances wholly unjustifiable. And the fight against it will never be stopped till the wrong is righted.

"And the only way to right it is to abolish the concession. Moving the line back to the original park boundary is only a compromise, and would not be a permanent cure. Make the park free; free to all on the same terms. This is exactly what the bill creating the park calls for and is exactly what the people want. Then why not let them have it?

"There is no problem confronting the American people today so serious as the transportation problem. And the chief source of all the trouble is bureaucratic control...And that same spirit of bureaucracy is gripping the Rocky Mountain National Park. There is too much bossism. There should be only such control as is necessary to protect the animals, the trees, the flowers, and streams. The mountains need no protection. Make the park in the fullest sense the people's playground.

"Up to the present time no restriction has been placed upon the entrance of private automobiles into this national park. Should this be done, it would place a burden upon thousands who are poorly able to bear it. It is a safe estimate to say that a tax of $5 per car would prevent hundreds of people in Larimer County alone from enjoying the park. And the park belongs to them as much as to the class more fortunate financially...What I am criticizing is the granting by a department of our Government, an exclusive franchise to one party to carry passengers into the Rocky Mountain National Park over roads built by the people for public use, and in many cases roads built decades before anyone had dreamed of such a thing as a national park. The personality of the agent that receives this concession is not of the slightest importance. It is the concession we criticize and not the agent, and this we shall continue to criticize until the concession is abolished and the roads given back to the people."

The question of the legality of monopolies in national parks was a tremendous significance in all those states where a park existed, for if the monopoly in Rocky Mountain National Park could be broken, it would establish a precedent, not desired by the National Park Service and the concessionaires who had become richly entrenched under government protection. Innumerable individuals were put in the field to combat Mills's propaganda, and personal attacks were made on his sincerity and veracity.

In December, 1920, Mills set forth "for the front." Papers in Kansas City, St. Louis, Des Moines, Houston, Dallas, Fort Worth, San Antonio, and many other Mid-Western and Southern cities spurred by his forcibly stated arguments came out with editorials and emphatic headlines condemning monopolies. The Texas Chamber of Commerce passed resolutions: "That it is the opinion of this body that Congress take appropriate steps to require the Secretary of the Interior to revoke all contracts giving exclusive privileges and permit competitive service to be reestablished in our national parks, and, the legislation be enacted that in future will prohibit the granting of exclusive privileges and provide that all rules and regulations promulgated by the Department of the Interior or park officials be subject to review by the courts."

The "Crusade," as one paper termed it, continued eastward, from Chicago to Pittsburgh, Cleveland, Columbus, New York, Springfield, and Boston, with continued publicity against monopolies. But it was not so easy as formerly to get a hearing. Everyone was glad to see him, to get his judgment on some state park site or local conservation project. When he put before them the need for immediate action to save national parks from too much bureaucracy, there was an evasive answer, or a suggestion that business was business, or that the proposition was too big to buck. Even those not fearless enough to take a definite stand were given something to think about, and their sympathies at least won by Mills's convincing arguments.

Among the numerous signed editorials by Clark McAdams, in the "St. Louis Post Dispatch," was the following, "Free Verse," February, 1921:

> Most of us submit tamely to injustice, feeling ourselves powerless to do anything about it.
>
> We are the meek, of whom it is said in the beatitudes that they shall inherit the earth.
>
> That may be true, but it isn't happening very fast.
>
> It may work out ultimately, but not now.
>
> Anyway, our old friend Enos Mills of Colorado is not like the rest of us.
>
> There is nothing meek about him.
>
> Apparently he doesn't believe the meek are going to get anywhere.
>
> He thinks the fierce, who hold the earth now, are going to continue in possession of it for a bit.
>
> Enos has a grievance.
>
> He came through here recently and told us about it.
>
> He says private monopolies in the national parks are defeating the purposes for which the parks are maintained.
>
> It costs $7.50 to take a private machine into Yellowstone Park, where millions of public money have been spent upon roads.
>
> There is not one of the national parks in which some privileged corporation has not gobbled up the transportation business and pretty much everything else that does the general coffers of monopoly fill.
>
> Enos is mighty mad about this.
>
> He thinks the parks should be free, since they belong to us.
>
> He thinks nobody ought to have the sole rights to anything.
>
> He says there isn't anything to the excuse that if someone is not given a monopoly the public will be deprived of adequate service.
>
> The parks have long since got past that, so he says.
>
> He knows all of us not having any special privilege in a national park think what he thinks about it, and therefore he takes his case to us.
>
> Pretty big order, you will say.
>
> It is, but Enos is not one of the meek.
>
> We have been watching his smoke.
>
> It rises everywhere like the white puffs of bombs

dropped from a circling plane.

Just about the time you think he is not getting to some quiet place on the landscape — Boom!

Or even Ba-a-a-a-a-a-a-n-n-n-n-n-g! when by a lucky shot he has hit an ammunition dump of the park bureaucrats.

The other day we saw that resolutions condemning private monopoly in national parks had been passed by the Texas Chamber of Commerce.

That followed a ringing protest against it in the New York press.

We knew by this sign Enos was a westward hoing, and we are watching now for a heluvan explosion in California.

He is a wonder.

That last is our text.

None of us who are of the meek is a wonder.

None of us will ever drive greed out of a national park or anywhere else.

None of us will ever arouse public opinion to correct anything.

It takes a man like Enos to do that.

Somebody who will go out like Paul Revere and rouse every Middlesex village and farm.

Somebody who can whoop, yell and stir things up generally.

Marse Henry Watterson, who went to Spain after the Spanish-American War, said the trouble with Spain was that she had no public opinion.

It is a wonderful thing if you have it, and it is a wonderful thing to be able to avail yourself of it.

This is what Enos is doing.

We give him three cheers.

A little man, but O my!

We cannot see how the new Secretary of the Interior can get around him.

It ought to be as Enos says it ought to be.

It ought to be as every newspaper and magazine and body of citizens appealed to anywhere says it ought to be.

And thanks to one man, hurling himself headlong at the foe and bidding all good men rise and abet him, we think it will be that way.

Pretty soon now.

Amen!

When Mills returned home, the active interest which he

had aroused somehow lagged. He followed his interviews of the winter with more printed statements and letters. But there seemed to be pressure brought to bear for those higher up. Much he wrote did not appear. Even his nature writings were suppressed in some quarters.

An almost complete censorship of the press on national park questions was being established. All the public were allowed to know came from official headquarters. One of the unfortunate outgrowths of the World War was the powerful machinery of propaganda built up in Washington and controlling, to a large extent, the entire country.

The campaign had one saving grace for Mills, he had faith in his cause, was sure of its justice, convinced of ultimate success. Once his beloved parks were placed on a free and equal basis, open to all, safe-guarded both from destruction and from private exploitation, he could rest on his accomplishment—he would have carried the noble cause on which he had enlisted through to completion.

He had no illusions in regard to the power of selfishness in ruling men's acts. But he received new and heightened insight into human nature, learned the length and depth of human inconstancy. Those who had been glad to stand up with him on the platform when the Rocky Mountain National Park celebration brought them into prominence, retreated to the other side of the platform now. If Mills had been dealing in personalities, he might have taken such change of heart more deeply. But he knew that the money being spent by the opposition could obtain all the supporters necessary from those willing to conform.

Another dictum of the times was the slogan, "It is unpatriotic to criticize the Government." When no good argument was available for not coming out in support of the issue, many so-called friends and former associates in conservation work thus defended their desertion.

Still another course was opened. The matter must be taken into the courts. A case was early filed. But this after dragging through many months was thrown out because "an individual cannot bring suit against the Government; as an individual, he is a part of that Government." Delays, hindrances, no decision, and the injustices to tourists going on increasingly, with park officials becoming more arrogant. Parks began to be looked upon with disfavor.

Other suits were filed, with more delay and no redress on the part of the Park officials. A summary of the legal aspects of the question are presented by Paul W. Lee, in the Appendix to Mills's "The Rocky Mountain National Park," setting forth the complexities of correcting evils or injustice in a national park through the court. Much public interest was aroused, for everyone realized the significance of a favorable decision.

So far as individual effort was concerned, this still devolved largely upon Mills. The world, as ever, was not keen for taking part in reform. These particular years were marked by a dark and low period of our national life, a curious atmosphere which followed upon the ending of the World War. The overwhelming majority of those financially independent was pleasure-bent and money-mad. It was an unfortunate time to try to awaken public sentiment. Moreover, the administration of President Harding, with Albert B. Fall as his first Secretary of the Interior, was not one in which to expect cooperation in purely altruistic, idealistic, enterprises.

Secretary Fall visited Estes Park, for the supposed purpose of adjusting the difficulties growing out of the monopolistic concession. Instead of making an effort to learn the nature of the complaints, he announced that he was tired of hearing about the Rocky Mountain National Park troubles and threatened to abolish the park altogether if complaints did not cease. And further he "approved, without qualifications, the policy of granting the transportation privileges to the Rocky Mountain Parks Transportation Company and condemned the constant agitation and criticism of the National Park Service policies."

In October, 1921, Mills made a two weeks' tour of Texas, at the request of those interested in having him pass upon desirable sites for state parks. He was asked to make as many lecture dates as the time would allow. Owing to interference with his mail and telegrams, and the constant circumventing of his plans, there was no correspondence beforehand, arrangements having been left to the judgment of a few friends, who maintained complete secrecy until the day the lecture was to be given. Before he had completed his tour of the State, pressure had been brought to bear on the various Chambers of Commerce to prevent his speaking.

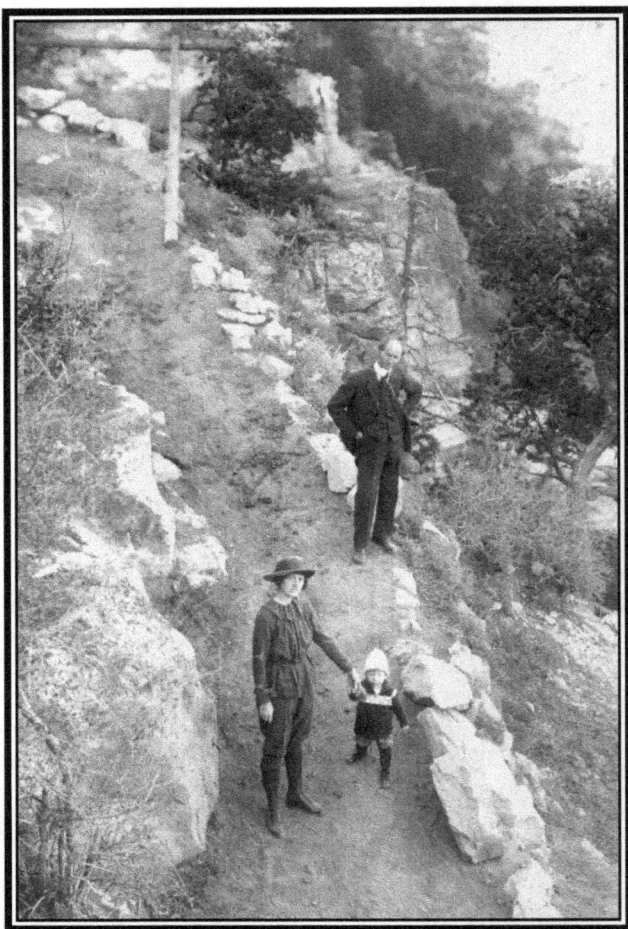

Enos with Esther and Enda at the
Grand Canyon during their Winter,
1921 trip through the Southwest.

Nevertheless, he got in an enormous amount of good work both for state and national parks.

In November, a trip was made to Los Angeles, where much misrepresentation of the monopoly question and Mills's attitude toward it had built up a strong defense for the National Park Service policies. Even though in the thick of the enemy's country he had several fine audiences both here and in San Diego. Sometimes the discussions became heated and even malicious, but Mills maintained his serenity, and emphasize the fact that it was the system of monopolies he was attacking and the highest good of the parks which he was defending.

It seemed as though everyone in the country must have heard of monopolies by this time, and been convinced, if they were accessible to reason, of the evils and abuses of bureaucracy. Mills planned another long lecture tour that was to take him all the way across the continent to Boston, at a time when he ought to have considered his personal comfort and well-being, and been permitted to savor the joys of home and family. He surely deserved a few months of peace in which to live in the scenes he loved and do the writing which he was so eminently fitted to do.

It was a strange fact that this man, who loved the solitude and the untouched charm of Nature, and who would willingly have spent his time entirely remote from most human contacts, yet hoped, worked, practically spent his life, to bring the great public into these far and secret places. His love for humanity was perhaps the mainspring of that endeavor.

One day, busy with his thoughts, he did not see the goggling eyes of a young waiter in a restaurant where he was having lunch between trains. The first thing that he knew, the boy's loaded tray emptied its contents of coffee, potatoes, meat, gravy, and fresh tomatoes into his lap. Mills naturally sprang to his feet, and the clatter of dishes brought the proprietor instantaneously to the scene. He was for dismissing the boy on the spot, but Mills, unperturbed, in his quiet, compelling voice, remonstrated, asking the boy, "How about it?"

With Mills seemingly not inclined to make a fuss, the boy recovered a little from the embarrassment of the situation and explained.

"Well, I'd seen Mr. Mills's picture in "The American Boy" so often and read all his stories, and I was so surprised to see him sitting there actual as life, I completely forgot what I was doing. But I'll pay for cleaning your suit, Mr. Mills, if you will let me."

Mills only laughed and told the boy he was glad to meet such an enthusiastic reader under any conditions.

Most of Mills's winter was devoid of humorous aspects. The important men in Washington with whom he had made appointments retreated behind the fortifications of bureaucracy. The national park monopoly question was being silenced by the powers that were endeavoring to fasten the monopoly upon the public. It was no longer "good form" to bring the matter up for discussion—everyone dodged it like a plague. When the Boston lecture date was canceled unceremoniously, a few days prior to his advertised appearance, Mills took it less as a personal affront than as an assault on liberty, an injustice to the cause of free speech.

He stayed on in New York, using his failures to reach the press and the platform as a convincing exposition, with those he reached in other ways, of the tremendous powers which a monopoly possessed. This persistent, personal presentation of the subject, allowing many false impressions to be privately corrected, probably did more good than any general public address.

In the subway one day, on his way to keep an important engagement, there was a collision between trains. Mills was caught in the wreck; numbers were injured, he among them. Giving little thought to the consequences, he hurried on to meet the man who had made this opportunity to see him. After the interview was over, he realized he was suffering.

The continued strain under which he had been for some time did not make recuperation easy. Mills returned to his home, doubtless thinking more strongly than ever that people should get out of the cities and into the safety zones of the wilderness. After all his narrow escapes on icy peaks and having been tumbled about on avalanches and buried in snow slides, to have to be laid up from a subway accident was almost humiliating.

On the way home he caught the flu which in his

weakened condition he was unable to throw off. To his friends he was as cheerful as ever, unwilling to arouse any solicitude. After a few weeks of rest, with the return of some of his former energy and all of his usual enthusiasm, he resumed his writing.

Summer came, the Inn opened as usual, Mills delegating many of the routine duties to his willing and numerous staff. He mingled among his guests with the same abundant interest in all their daily activities on the trail. If any suggestion was made that he should take more rest and let the guests look after themselves, he only smiled his appreciation. Throughout the summer he continued his evening lectures, unwilling to any detail of entertainment should be missed.

For two years Mills had been endeavoring to enlist the support of the State of Colorado in asserting its authority on the state-built roads in the Rocky Mountain National Park. In August, 1922, this was finally accomplished, Governor Oliver H. Shoup filing a brief in behalf of the State of Colorado against the Department of the Interior, contesting the legality to the exclusive transportation concession granted by the Government for which Mills agreed to pay the expense of litigation. It would only be a question of a few months, Mills felt assured, before the traveling public would be restored to the happy freedom of national parks, freed from arbitrary regulations which now made "their fullest enjoyment" impossible.

It was well for Mills that he could not foresee the seven years more of legal and legislative controversy which were to ensue before the citizens of Colorado succumbed under the pressure from Washington, and relinquish their own and the nation's rights to personal liberty in the national parks of the State—Mesa Verde and the Rocky Mountain National Parks. Inconceivable as it may seem, the Colorado Legislature ceded an inalienable right (police power), which, under our Constitution and the decisions of the United States Supreme Court, cannot legally be transferred, except by an amendment to the Colorado Constitution, calling for a constitutional convention.

Mills rested happy in the thought that his cause would soon be won. The suit filed by the State of Colorado would bring the question of monopoly of national park roads to early and successful decision. The case was clear, it only required the necessary hearing to have the controversy ended. This was just a month before Mills's death. Without his realizing it, the necessary trip to Denver and legal consultations had taken his last bit of energy.

"Enos Mills is dead." So the headlines in the nation's papers said, September 21, 1922. It did not seem possible, but the sad news was true. Mills had finished his work; the last story was written, the last letter signed, the last word said for his beloved parks. He went quietly, as though he might have turned a bend in the trail, leaving others to follow along his path among the things he loved. Although only fifty-two years of age, he had lived several lives coincidentally, and had made each of them count for more than that of the average man with one line of endeavor. Measured by Muir's maxim—"Longest is the life that contains the largest amount of work that is a steady delight"—he had lived immeasurably. He had really lived!

A touching tribute was paid Enos Mills in the assemblage gathered in the great living room of the Inn for the funeral, three days later; there were people of all ages and every rank of society or professional endeavor; those who had known him in his youth, and those who had come to know him at the height of his fame; dear friends from near and far, and those others, so-called enemies, with their deeds of malice forgiven and forgotten.

The service was as simple as the life of the man for whom it was held. Passages from the books which had influenced Mills's life were read, touched with the sweet breath of nature which had been his own breath of life. As the Sunset hour gathered the clouds and glory above Long's Peak, and the harvest of aspen leaves made gold the yard about his home, Mills's favorite lines which he had applied to his beloved nature, were spoken:

> "When old age shall this generation waste,
> Thou shalt remain, in midst of other woe
> Than ours, a friend to man, to whom thou say'st,
> 'Beauty is truth, truth beauty,—that is all
> Ye know on earth, and all ye need to know.'"

The last photograph taken of Enos, September, 1922.

Appendix
Tributes

The people of Colorado and of the whole country mourn at the loss of a man who has given so much of his life and wonderful ability to their interests and welfare as has Mr. Mills. He was an outstanding figure in American life, especially as a naturalist, and through his great ability, intense earnestness and energy, he has brought out to the world as no other person has the interesting and instructive life of the wilds of our great Rockies, and presented them in a most entertaining way to the whole world. Such services are invaluable to mankind and it is because of those services, as well as because of the character of the man himself, that I beg to express this feeling of deepest regret, upon behalf of all of the people, that we have had to lose him.

(Signed) OLIVER H. SHOUP
Governor

If Enos Mills had lived in a city he would have spent himself trying to reform it and fighting the people's battles. Fortunate for him and the West, which he loved passionately and understandingly, he had within him the soul of the Pioneer. He gave his thought and his reforming instinct, which was very strong in him, toward the preservation of Nature. His fame had spread widely.

The preservation of the works bestowed by Nature upon the West was his great endeavor. To him it was a religion and he pursued it as such. He wore himself out fighting for God's handiwork against those that would trade in it. First of all he engaged himself in having Congress create the Rocky Mountain National Park. He knew all the ground and what it contained. He had the faculty of making others see it almost as he saw it. After the park was created he did not like the way bureaucracy was doing with it from Washington and he took up the cudgels for the freedom of all the national parks. Whether he was right or wrong he believed in his cause and was without ulterior motives.

Estes Park and the name of Enos Mills were inseparably linked. Something distinctive has been taken out of the heart of the Rocky Mountains. He was, if the phrase may be permitted, a natural naturalist. He wrote of what he observed in his long tramps through the mountains in summer and winter. He has joined a band of noble brothers on the other side of the range.

"The Rocky Mountain News," editorial, September 22, 1922

The cause of nature protection sustains an irreparable loss in the death of its ablest and most ardent advocate. The stimulus which Enos A. Mills gave to Nature-study and a promotion of the love of all that is beautiful in scenery, in plant and animal life, is beyond estimate. He was the John Muir, Burroughs and Thoreau of Colorado and the Rocky Mountain region. However much I appreciate his great works on Nature, I shall miss him though more as a personal friend and a strong supporter of the work I have been attempting at the State Museum.

ELLSWORTH BETHEL
The State Historical and Natural History Society of Colorado

To adequately tell the story of Enos Mills, one should follow the trails he traced into high, silent and lonely places, for if ever a person partook of the qualities of his environment this lover of nature, friend of beasts and birds, grim, unarmed warrior, was he.

While other young men were caught in the turmoil of industrial and profession activities, Enos Mills was staking a homestead for himself at the foot of Long's Peak and beginning those explorations on foot which made the region as familiar to him as a primer is to a child.

With John Muir and John Burroughs, Enos Mills will form the trinity of America's great naturalists who gave Nature's story a form of which man, woman and child could understand and love.

FRANCES WAYNE
"The Denver Post," September 22, 1922

AN APPRECIATION

Like all great men, Enos Mills was perhaps least appreciated while he lived—and however much that appreciation was—I think all will agree that Mills, his work and what he stood for, cannot be too much known and understood. It means far more to our children than the work of men after whom many of our mountain peaks have been named. Some of these men like Zebulon Pike, discovered the bodies of our mountains. Mills discovered their souls. In the sordid struggle of commercialism largely to enrich themselves, men have discovered their mineral wealth. Mills discovered there a far greater wealth—one that may be shared with all mankind. He found there the sweet stories of the trees, the romance of the woods, and all living creatures that inhabit those temples of God. He had brought them to light through marvelous understanding, he did this in his lectures and happily in the books he has left us and our children. Here we may find the real poetry, music and philosophy of life. Or, rather, here we may find the touchstone, the inspiration, the way to Heaven on earth. His insight and understanding of life as it is, as interpreted through God's living things, will make for us a better citizenship.

Let us resolve that the soul of those mountains shall not be commercialized by the touch of men's greed that broke his heart. Let us make the start now by declaring a Mills's Day in all our schools where we may reach the unsullied souls of little children with the noble heart of Enos Mills—the heart that is the heart of the hills, the soul of nature, the touch of God.

JUDGE BEN B. LINDSEY

A big man lies dead at Long's Peak. Big in deeds of human service.

Not great at all, in ways of bloody valor. Not a "hero" with a long list of slain. Not a huntsman with many crimson notches on his rifle stock.

And yet—he was a gallant fighter, for the preservation of LIFE. He was a brave soldier, in the ARMY of the COMMON GOOD.

I am tempted to put a broad band of mourning around this little appreciation. To emphasize Colorado's loss.

But mourning would not have appealed to Enos Mills. He despised ostentation. He loved simplicity. He feared nothing.

So why mourn?

Instead, let us be grateful that such a man lived among us, all these years. And taught us to KNOW Colorado. The real Colorado. Nature's Colorado.

Let us be grateful for the plucky fight he made, successfully, to save Rocky Mountain Park as a National recreation spot, for all time.

Not forgetting, either, that other fight in which he was engaged when he died—the fight against the curse of monopoly in the park.

His great legacy we share with the world. For he gave it while he lived. In his books and his wide personal contact.

"The Denver Express," September 21, 1922

Mr. Mills endeared himself to me by his constant defense of things Western. He loathed the Nature-faker and those who wrote and spoke with no authority on the great West.

The regrettable thing is, the mantle of Enos A. Mills will not fall on the shoulders of anyone. The field which he occupied is vacant—our mountains have no one who spoke with such perfect authority.

ANDY ADAMS
COLORADO SPRINGS, September, 1922

Mills was one of the most famous outdoor men in America, had climbed all over the Rocky Mountains alone and unarmed, had ascended Long's Peak more than three hundred times, had demonstrated in a thousand emergencies his calm nerves and cool head. Yet a trip in the New York subway was his doom.... It is doubtful if the death of any other man in Colorado would leave a greater gap. It is as if a mountain peak had sunk below the horizon.

THOMAS HARDY

I came to know Enos Mills as one of the noblest of men and truest of friends, whose untimely passing will be received with profound regret by the many thousands throughout this country and abroad who delighted in his invaluable contributions to the literature of nature. Mr. Mills was a great man in a very real sense, gifted for useful and honorable service as few men are, and his life work is a benefaction to mankind. He impressed his name indelibly upon the history of his age.

He had the brave and dauntless spirit of the pioneer, the serene and contemplative mind of a philosopher and the soul and vision of a poet. His passionate love of nature inspired all that was elevated in thought, generous in impulse, pure in morals and beautiful in sentiment.

He walked among the peaks and set his name among the stars. He was the living spirit of the Rockies, the articulate voice of nature, and he interpreted her in all her moods with all the fervor of his poetic imagination.

We tramped the mountainsides together and he told me wondrous stories of the Rockies. Where he stood there is now vast emptiness and solemn silence, and where we stand there is deep heartache and sincere mourning. No one can ever take his place. He was unique and stood alone, matchless in his simplicity and grandeur as the inspired interpreter of the Rockies and the radiant incarnation of their majesty and glory.

EUGENE V. DEBS

One of marks of genius is an independent soul. There was the freedom of genius in Enos Mills. It was because Enos Mills belonged in what he called "The Rocky Mountain Wonderland" that he was able to recreate the wild life so vividly for a multitude of people whose only acquaintance with it came through his fascinating writing. He was a powerful force in creating public sentiment for the splendid preserves of wild life and scenery known as the national parks. But the man was more than his achievements. He brought a fresh view of live to all who came in contact with him. In his death the country loses a rare personality.

"The Kansas City Star," September 22, 1922

Enos Mills was one of those men, few in number but fascinating in personality, who help to keep alive the love of nature in the hearts of sympathetic readers. In his field of activity—the mountains—he stood without rivals. His untimely death will be regretted not only by his readers, but more particularly by those who met him in his own haunts and looked through his eyes at the wonders of the great hills. For these latter his influence will by no means cease at his death.

"The Baltimore (Md.) Sun"

All American boys are bereaved by Mr. Mills's death. Beyond measurement are the pleasures and benefits they have gained from the eloquently simple stories which Mr. Mills wrote of his unique experiences and keen, accurate observations of the marvelous world outdoors. These stories, published first for the boys of today, will be read with enjoyment and benefit by other boys through innumerable years. A heritage of this kind and a recollection of the sort of man he was, justifies a pride in him all of us who knew Mr. Mills will ever cherish.

"The American Boy Magazine"

In company with a large part of the Nation, Sunset Magazine sorrows in the loss of Enos Mills. In him, the West lost one of its most valuable sons.

"The Sunset Magazine"

As I watch the last bright rays of the September sun disappearing over the hills that border the far shore of Lake Sebago I am thinking of the sadness which lovers of nature and conservators of natural beauty must feel because of the death of Enos A. Mills at Long's Peak, Colorado.

Mr. Mills was known throughout the English speaking world for his books and countless articles in magazines and newspapers. He was a man of one subject, of one enthusiasm. His entire life was devoted to the study of the wild creatures and flowers of the American forests. At sixteen years of age he built himself a cabin near the place where he died—this cabin was his laboratory, but all the Rockies was his stamping ground.

J. W. F.
"Philadelphia Public Ledger"

Enos A. Mills was one of the most beloved men in Colorado. As an outdoor naturalist, guide, explorer and lover of nature-study, he incorporated his varied and interesting experiences in several volumes that gave him a state, national and international reputation. He was not a scientist of the laboratory, unless all the outdoors of mountain and plain be so considered. Scientific terms and analysis found no place in his several publications. His study and observations concerned the living mammal, bird, reptile, and flower. His was a naturalist and guide who did not carry a gun. His volumes will always remain as part of the "Life History" of the flora and fauna of Colorado.

"The Rocky Mountain Herald"

Mr. Mills joined the Colorado Mountain Club at its very beginning and was always interested in its work. Through his lectures and writings he did more than any other man to make the Colorado Rockies known the public of the United States. He devoted his life to conservation as he saw it, and here is where he made some of his bitterest enemies. By teaching and example he was one of the first to advocate flower preservation and forest protection, and his pages are full of pleas for the lives of the birds and the harmless animals of our mountains. Latterly his stories taught thousands of boys, large and small, to hunt with a camera instead of a gun. This influence for good alone has been a wide-spread blessing, and has done a world of good that will live long after his name becomes dim. To scores of Mountain Club members he was a warm personal friend, and his loss will be keenly felt.

"Colorado Mountain Club"

Comparative Obituaries
including typographical errors

"Estes Park Trail" Friday, September 22, 1922

ENOS A. MILLS, AUTHOR, NATURE GUIDE AND PIONEER OF ESTES PARK DEPARTS FROM THIS LIFE

At 2:30 Thursday morning the great white angel called at the home of Enos A. Mills, far famed author, naturalist and mountaineer, at his cottage at Longs Peak Inn and he departed this life in the flesh and the company of his wife and baby daughter and of his friends and acquaintances all over the land. The end came very suddenly and his going was entirely unexpected by his friends.

Since early last winter when injured in a subway wreck Mr. Mills had not been in the best of health, but his friends had not fully realized his true condition. At the time of the wreck two ribs were broken and punctured the lungs, causing the formation of pus sacks. Upon his return to his home in the Park in January this year he was stricken by a severe attack of influenza, from which he never fully recovered. Recently he has suffered severely from abscesses on the jaw and at the roots of the teeth. Only ten days ago a portion of the jaw was removed and also several of the teeth. However, the poison had penetrated the body, resulting in his sudden going Thursday morning.

Enos A. Mills was born in Kansas in 1870 and came to this state at the age of fourteen. He came to the Park while still a lad and secured his first job in the Park washing dishes at the Elkhorn Lodge. For the past thirty years he has spent much of his time exploring the Rockies, studying wild animal life, in extensive travel and in the writing of numerous books, most of which were published by Doubleday, Paige & Co. and by Houton-Mifflin. Mr. Mills was the father of the Rocky Mountain National Park, the most popular National Park in America today and established Longs Peak Inn, a hotel near the base of Longs Peak, that proved quite popular with many tourists.

In August of 1918 Mr. Mills was united in marriage with Miss Esther A. Burnell, a homesteader on the Fall River road in Estes Park, and a daughter came to bless the home.

In addition to his wife and daughter, Mr. Mills leaves a brother and mother, residing at Fort Scott, Kans., a sister, Mrs. Ella H. Hart, Goodman Kans., and his brother Joe Mills of Estes Park.

While funeral arrangements have not been made public, the many friends feel that as a fitting close for his career nothing could be better arranged than that his body should lie at rest in the land he so greatly loved and of which he was so proud.

The many friends of Mr. Mills all unite in extending their heartfelt sympathy to the bereaved ones.

———

Simple funeral services will be held at the Inn Sunday afternoon at 4:30 o'clock. It has been requested that no flowers be sent.

"The Loveland Reporter", Thursday, September 21, 1922

ENOS MILLS AUTHOR-NATURALIST
DIES TODAY AT ESTES PARK HOME
WORLD FAMED AUTHOR PASSES AWAY AND PEN IS FOREVER
STILLED, WAS ONE OF THE MOST PICTURESQUE FIGURES IN
HISTORY OF THE GREAT WEST, LOVED THE MOUNTAINS

Enos Mills, age 52, author of many books and one of the world's famous naturalists, died at his home at Estes Park, Longs Peake, this morning, death being due to heart failure. He was injured in a subway accident in New York city two years ago and never fully recovered from the injuries.

He was born at Fort Scott, Kas., and came to the Rockies when 14 years old, erecting his little log cabin, which still stands within the shadows of Longs Peak. He spent practically all his life roughing it in the mountains and writing books about the great outdoors. Among his books of note are "Wild Life in the Rockies," "The Story of a Thousand Year Pine," and "Watched by Wild Animals."

He was married in 1918 at Des Moines, Ia., to Miss Esther D. Burnell, who, with a three-year-old daughter, Enda, survive him.

There will be no formal funeral service and the body will rest near the scene of his last work at Longs Peak...

ENOS MILLS DIES AT LONGS PEAK
HEART BROKEN BY PARK INVADERS
FAMOUS NATURALIST WAS THE
'FATHER OF ROCKY MOUNTAIN NATIONAL PARKS"
(By Francis Wayne)

Enos Abijah Mills, father of the Rocky Mountain National park, one of the world's great naturalists, woke from sleep in his room at Longs Peak inn at 4 o'clock Friday morning, called for his wife and before she could reach him sank into his pillows and died.

Of heart failure, according to the technical verdict of science.

Of heart break, according to the friends of Enos Mills, who watched the undaunted fight he made thru many years —first to induce the federal congress to create a National park of the region dominated by Longs peak and then against the commercialization of nature and what he considered an unwarranted and evil monopoly of transportation into and thru Estes park.

To adequately tell the story of Enos Mills, one should follow the trails he traced into high, silent and lonely places, for if ever a person partook of the qualities of his environment this lover of nature, friend of beasts and birds, grim, unharmed warrior, was he.

Little is known of the forbears of Enos Mills. Born in Kansas City, Kan., April 22, 1870, son of Enos and Ann Mills, who probably been of those pioneers who dreading crowds kept ever a few paces ahead of towns and cities.

Early in life young Mills came to Colorado, not pausing to find him a place in the valleys, but going straight to the region which must forever be associated with his name and efforts.

While other young men were caught in the turmoil of industrial and professional activities, Enos Mills was staking a homestead for himself at the foot of Longs peak and beginning those explorations on foot which made the region as familiar to him as a primer is to a child.

Winter and summer, a pack tossed over his shoulder, with no firearms to protect him from wild beasts, because to him no beasts were wild or unfriendly, Mills climbed the snow-covered mountains and delved deep into the secrets of nature.

"All of one winter I never heard another human voice than

my own." he said when explaining himself to an interviewer. "Yet I was not lonely, because the squirrels and chipmunks, even the great grizzlies— noblest of the beasts—and bob cats talked to me as friends and brothers. And as for the birds and the pines, they, too, have a language which the attuned ear may understand and enjoy."

WROTE STORY OF PINE ON SOLITARY TRIP.

On one of those solitary journeys into vast spaces Mills procured his material for the memorable "Story of a Thousand Year Pine," wherein, standing in its centuries old place on the mountain, the tree, looking back, narrates what has happened to itself and to man in those thousand years.

Since all living creatures were his friends, Mills neither could nor would take the life of any, and so when he unfolded his pack for the night's rest or set a camp from which he would start his explorations, he took out his box of provisions, consisting of nuts and chocolate, and so subsisted.

For two years he served the government as official snow observer, and then he became aware that perhaps he had a message which the outside world might care to hear.

This message was to the effect that it was the duty of the government of the United States to take over the area dominated by Longs peak and set it aside as a national park reserve.

The difficulty confronting Mills was that he had been silent so long, his only arguments being with his dumb friends whom he met by the wayside or induced to nest near his tent or in the eaves of the cabin he had built.

When he had left home in Kansas he had but the rudiments of an education.

But he had taken with him a bible, given by his mother, and had acquired the writings of John Burroughs and John Muir and had enriched the soil of a naturally acquisitive mind with what they had to say.

So Enos Mills, locking the door of his cabin, came into the world of living, bustling, competing men and women and in a stammering, halting, wondering way took them by storm with the message he brought.

Within a year after his first appearance at the Denver Woman's club, when in ill-fitting suit, his blue eyes peering out into the auditorium, his hair standing straight above the bald space like a halo, he asked the cooperation of the club women of Colorado to procure a national park, every woman's club of importance in the country was vieing for his presence.

Also magazine editors hearing of the timid, quiet voiced naturalist with a new twist to an old story, made bids for his production, and soon Enos Mills, from being an obscure snow observer of Longs Peak, became a character of national distinction.

Meantime Estes park had attracted the attention of hundreds of tourists and scores of builders of summer homes and hotels. It became necessary for Mills to work swiftly if the region was not to be invaded by railroads and taken over by the emissaries of greed.

To win the press, and so on a time he invited a number of editors to be his guests in Estes park. They accepted. Each has said the evening before the open hearth, with its burning logs, in the long, dimly lighted living room of the hotel will not be forgotten. A good supper had been enjoyed. Cigars and pipes were lighted. Lamps were dimmed.

Mills, leaning against the side of the mantel, began to talk of his experiences in the park when no other kept him company. He told of his innumerable climbs of the austere peak and of the glory of what lay round about and beyond and of how forever and forever the land and all it held should be set apart for the pleasure and education of the people. Being a man unsophisticated in the ways of the world, he spoke straight from the heart and into the hearts of his guests.

And the press of Colorado got behind Enos Mills in his far-visioned project to have congress create a Rocky Mountain National park. And it was done.

In his leisure time Mills had built the Longs Peak inn, which became and is the mecca for what is known as the intelligentsia of the land who seek the west in the summer time. And there in the long foyer, built of pines with vast fireplace always aglow, many of the nation's distinguished writers and publicists have met in conference. It was the Roycroft of the Rocky Mountains with Enos Mills as presiding genius, until three years ago, when, having married Miss Esther A. Burnell, he shared honors with his wife.

But Mills, with all his success, was to know the bitterness of defeat. For, in accordance with economic law, there came a demand for adequate transportation facilities into and out of the park. A corporation was achieved which supplied freight and passenger motor service.

All other concerns were barred. This was to Mills idealistic nature a violation, not alone of honesty, but of decency. Amazed as he would have been if one of his grizzly friends had turned and bitten him, Mills began to argue for the establishment of a competitive system. It should be every man's right to carry passengers and freight into the Rocky Mountain National park.

He appealed to women's clubs to throw their influence in his favor. He appealed to chambers of commerce and men's social and civic organizations; he appealed finally to courts and to congress, and one by one thumbs went down.

It was the failure to win a fight he regarded as just that first began to break the spirit and tell on the heart of Enos Mills.

In January he went to New York to lecture and to discuss future work with his publishers, always avid for the product of his pen, and there he was injured in a subway collision. What injuries he suffered were said to be slight but nerves, already overtaxed, paid the penalty.

He returned home less buoyant, less interested in life than when he went away. This summer he actively participated in the management of the Longs Peak Inn with a hope always in the back of his mind that he might effect a sale of the property this year and thus be able to retire to quieter surroundings to devote himself to writing. Perhaps in his thought was a sense of man's ingratitude to a faithful servant and defender, for to everyone to whom he talked at all intimately Mills would, after the first greetings speak of the monopoly which had invaded the park and denounce it as a shame.

One of his most prosperous seasons was drawing to an end when Enos Mills died, in his fifty-second year.

Of heart failure, the scientists say.

Of heart break, his friends believe.

Death came as he had often said he hoped it would come, with quiet dignity.

With John Muir and John Burroughs Enos Mills will form the trinity of America's great naturalists who gave Nature's story a form which man, woman and child could understand and love.

Surviving him are his widow, Esther B. Mills, his daughter Enda, 3 years old, two brothers, Joseph Mills of Estes Park and William Mills of Fort Scott, Kan., and a sister, Mrs. Ella M. Hart of Goodland, Mo.

"New York Tribune," September 22, 1922

A Nature Pioneer

No mean place on the roll of benefactors of the nation is filled by the name of Enos A. Mills, explorer and naturalist. There were few more indefatigable explorers of the wonderland of the Rocky Mountains and few who did so much as he, by personal guidance and otherwise, to acquaint the multitudes of tourists with the really worthwhile features of that region.

His best work was done as one of the founders of the series of national parks in the Far West and as an educator of the public in the desirability of conserving the native flowers, trees and animals of the wilds. To him was due much of the credit for the enactment of laws and rules for the protection of plants, birds and beasts. As a lover and student of nature and an expositor of her charms and wonders he was a not unworthy successor of Audubon and Thoreau and colleague of Muir and Burroughs.

It was a strange freak of fate that a man who had challenged death a thousand times in his lonely scramblings among the cliffs and peaks of the Rocky Mountains, and who scorned the protection of firearms against grizzly bears and mountain lions, should receive in a New York subway the injuries which ended his active and useful life. Perhaps remembrance of that circumstance may cause New Yorkers to regard with more sympathy the interests, so remote from this city, to which he devoted his career.

HILDEGARDE HAWTHORNE OSKISON
EAST RIDGE
RIDGEFIELD, CONNECTICUT

June 29,'49

Dear Mrs. Mills:

I have been away for a week and have only just found your
letter in regard to possibility of a new edition of the book
on Enos Mills. No, I had seen no mention of the burning of the
Hall, where I had so many times in the past. I deeply regret it's
destruction. Neither was I aware of your having sold the Inn.
A lovely era has passed.

I too regretted receiving the notice from Houghton Mifflin about
ending the publication of our book. I do not think there is much
chance of their starting it again. They may even have destroyed
the plates. Also, I think that you will have more influence on
their decision since you are in touch with the publicity in the
west regarding what has happened. I have seen no account of it in
the New York papers, or at least in the Tribune, to which I
subscribe.

I am therefore enclosing the contract, and shall write them to
that effect. I will of course say that it seems to me it would be
a fine thing to have the book appear. I release the contract to you,
therefore, and will hope for the best.

It is a pleasure to hear that your daughter, Enda, the little charming
girl I knew once, is married and with children of her own.

Consider the copy-right interests as your own, for if there is a new
edition it will owe its rebirth to you.

Sincerely yours,

Hildegarde Hawthorne Oskison